WEDNESDAY WRITERS

As we travel
life on Planet Earth
together, we are all
lessons for each other.
Cheers,
Kathleen Faraday

WEDNESDAY WRITERS

10 years of writing women's lives

THE WOMEN WRITERS' WORKSHOP

EDITED BY
ELIZABETH FISHEL
&
TERRI HINTE

WITH A PREFACE BY
ELIZABETH FISHEL

Harwood Press
Oakland, California

Harwood Press
6134 Harwood Avenue
Oakland, CA 94118

Cover art: Mary-Jo Murphy
Cover design: Andreas Jones

Printed in U.S.A.

First printing: March 2003

LIBRARY OF CONGRESS CATALOGING-IN-PUBLICATION DATA

Writers'Workshop, Women.
   Wednesday writers: 10 years of writing women's lives /
   Women Writers'Workshop ... [et al.]. — 1st ed.
      p. cm.
   ISBN 0-9728110-0-1
   I. Title.

                              2003101575

In memory
of
June Anne Baker
and
Lorna C. Mason

CONTENTS

PREFACE

Elizabeth Fishel

EVERY WEDNESDAY MORNING for the past ten years, twelve or so women and I have gathered in my living room to write about our lives. In other worlds we may be doctors and lawyers, therapists and publicists, mothers taking a break from raising children to probe our own thoughts. We may have written briefs and reports, manuals or lengthy letters but not yet claimed our own voice, clarified our own vision. But here, sinking comfortably into armchairs and sofa, sipping strong coffee or peppermint tea, we are linked as writers, exploring the mysteries of our lives, airing and sharing our dreams and doubts, learning to write from the heart. Together we create personal essays and memoirs, poems and short fiction, op-ed pieces and newspaper columns. This anthology, *Wednesday Writers*, presents the best of ten years of writing on the things we care about most passionately: identity and memory, love and loss, family across the generations, health and politics, the daily pleasures and surprises of ordinary life.

Sitting in our circle are women from their twenties to their seventies writing about every life-stage—from starting a first job to reflecting on a long, complicated career, from raising toddlers and guiding children through school to rejoicing in grandchildren and making peace with parents long gone. Often women are drawn to the group to make sense of life passages and upheavals, to use the steady unflinching gaze of introspection to uncover resilience. These may be personal passages (long-married to suddenly single, longtime parent to empty-nester, carefree healthy to facing illness) as well as creative passages (lawyer to writer, daily journal-keeper to published author). Sharing our work with each other, week after week, month after month over these ten years, we have seen our stories gain depth and resonance from being part of a writers' community.

Every week the group spotlights one or two members' pieces. We applaud the golden lines, memorable descriptions so particular to each writer's experience that no one else could have written them. We also give thoughtful suggestions to help each piece become the best it can be. Every piece in this book was workshopped this way and later revised, for a willingness to be a re-writer is another hallmark of the Wednesday Writers.

Each of us keeps her own writer's journal, perhaps a small notebook tucked handily inside a purse to catch inspiration on line at the supermarket or carpooling the kids. The group also keeps a journal together, each woman taking turns writing in it, week by week. The cover of our first group journal was a fan quilt, a fitting image for the piecing together of our stories, the scraps and remnants of our lives. Our journal has become a reservoir for story ideas, character sketches, reflections on the seasons of our lives, a place to ferret out and preserve those treasures Virginia Woolf called "diamonds in the dustheap." Sometimes our journal entries muse on the act of writing itself for sooner or later every journal reflects inward in a circular pattern, its own mandala. Highlights from our journal and our reflections on the writing life are also an important part of this book and we hope an inspiration to other writers.

Although the focus of our group is on process not product, we're proud that some of our work has been published in Bay Area and national publications. Among the pieces reprinted here are a prize-winning travel essay by Terri Hinte, timely opinion pieces by Rina Alcalay and Gina Waldman, a parenting essay by Michelle Wells Grant, a humor column by Ronnie Caplane, and a bimonthly newspaper column, "Double Talk," created and co-written by Kathleen Faraday, Robin Slovak, and Joan Stevenson, none of whom, by the way, had ever published before joining the group.

Wednesday Writers is the culmination of a tradition first suggested by June Baker, who was the editor of our first class anthology many years ago. The present anthology was inspired by the courageous writers among us, including June, who have faced cancer and shared their writing about it with the group. We dedicate this book to their spirit. Proceeds from *Wednesday Writers* will be donated in their honor to the Carol Franc Buck Breast Care Center at the University of California at San Francisco Comprehensive Cancer Center, a program of the National Center of Excellence in Women's Health.

To order additional copies of *Wednesday Writers* or for more information about the Wednesday writers' group, contact erfishel@hotmail.com.

WE GRATEFULLY ACKNOWLEDGE the support of the Auxiliary at UCSF Medical Center at Mount Zion. Founded in 1887, the Auxiliary has continuously served the community both as a volunteer and philanthropic organization. It has evolved into a dedicated provider of services and financial assistance to numerous patient programs available at the UCSF Medical Center at Mount Zion, including many that are now being offered through the recently opened state-of-the-art UCSF Comprehensive Cancer Center and the National Center of Excellence in Women's Health. The Auxiliary's annual membership campaign, tribute funds, gift shop, Friend to Friend Store, and fund-raisers all provide needed monetary resources to further such successful programs as Art For Recovery, Cancer Center Support Groups, pediatric services and supplies, and on-campus patient Resource Centers, as well as transportation and accommodations for low-income patients and their families. For more information about the Auxiliary, visit their Web site: http://mountzion.ucsfmedicalcenter.org/auxiliary/

THE WRITING LIFE

SOMETHING THAT MATTERS

Charli Depner

IT IS THE WOMAN WRITER'S version of Pergonal. Each week I leave the Women's Writing Workshop with an optimistic image of follicles budding, releasing a profusion of the eggs we were born with. Encased in each are worlds lost or imagined, exquisite moments, treasured memories. The workshop cherishes these seeds and nurtures them with validation, willful determination, and the imperative to tell our stories.

Together, we strive for something elusive—to, as Audre Lorde put it, "touch something that matters." It excites me that our words attend to things that have gone unseen, unappreciated, things that one must pause to savor.

I sought out the group as I began to make sense of the way my peculiar brand of motherhood was transforming my life. As a social scientist, I had been trained to write as an objective observer. This mode was not touching what mattered, not informing things in which I was deeply immersed. I was writing around the issue, assuming the various postures of the blind men on the elephant. There was no truth in stepping out of the action to take a look, since the vantage point was not mine. What sought expression was inside the beast.

The way I wanted to write was more like a craft, like the pots that women make from the clay beneath their feet or the quilts that represent new ways of combining appealing remnants gathered over a lifetime. This kind of work requires an act of faith. A woman weaving a kilim is not constrained by a design plan. Insight emerges from the process of being with her art. She trusts a creative force to guide the laying down of each strand, until the pattern takes form.

Though craft is a woman's tradition, for most of our history, words have been a prohibited medium. We gather to support each other, certainly; but it is more than that. Often I feel that my story is deeply embedded in the shared experience of the diverse group of women seated with me in Elizabeth's magically luminous living room. We were raised with different notions about what mattered about being a woman and have survived tricky twists and turns in the definition of our roles. Each of us has something unique to say about where she has traveled and what she has found there. The stories feel connected in a way that I do not fully understand. There is a palpable feeling of resonance when one of us manages to "touch what matters" and a gentle prodding when more work is required.

Elizabeth has subtly crafted a weekly ritual that seems to mirror the way writing works itself into my life—an interweaving of personal meaning, shared experience, inspiring work, and an iterative process of revelation. Gradually we weave each other into our lives, sharing poems, disappointments, triumphs, and secrets.

Like other crafts, this writing lacks validation. (I worry less about the subject matter—I trust women to activate interest in what is being told. What we need most is to fight against the forces that have silenced the telling.) It is difficult to accept a process that is necessarily erratic, didactically recursive. It is difficult to respect notes scribbled on sales slips, studded with the feathery gum that resides only in the bottom of a purse. It is difficult to write about a life that unpredictably intrudes with tummy aches and protracted bedtimes. Yet this feels like the way to touch what matters; the weekly workshop sustains it and gives us a glimpse of what is possible.

From the class journal.

BOOK BUILDING

Wendy Scott Bertrand

AT THE FIRST WEDNESDAY MEETING, I stated my commitment to a thousand words a day on a memoir about being an architect. Not a famous architect, or the exceptional woman architect, but one of the many architects working day by day to highlight the opportunities for quality in the building of places. Generally our work is relatively unknown and, along with many other occupations, undervalued. The idea of telling my story came to me as I decided to think realistically about getting boxes of college work, project contract drawings, reports, publications, job applications, employee evaluations, letters, and essays in order to send them to the International Archive of Women in Architecture in Blacksburg, Virginia.

After three weeks of tapping keys at a thousand words per day, I panicked. I couldn't visualize my book as a whole. Here I was generating text from my college experience, world travels, project files from three federal agencies, notes on organizational culture, management style, feminist issues of the day, and records of professional activities, when I thought, "This was so much effort without the conceptual planning and design that I would routinely put into a project before preparing production drawings. I better get a writing coach to help me funnel my production of text into meaningful chapters." I mentioned my fears to Elizabeth, our workshop leader. In her soft consistent manner, she immediately placed the concern in the hands of the writing group. Calm voices assured me that this "generating stage" was appropriate and necessary to move from my archives to the page. Elizabeth followed with the suggestion that I use a bulletin board and post-it notes to capture pivotal events and themes as they steamed up.

Around the fourth week of twelve sessions, my friends were asking about my new rigorous commitment to writing—every morning was taken. I felt unsure how to respond. So on the next Wednesday I asked how others in the group shared their writing experiences with outsiders. From around the circle came motives, reactions, pointers, and tears. Each of us can be vulnerable to arrows of criticism and gems of encouragement. If writers are happy to be writing, do friends need to know? Maybe not. When someone asks, "What are you writing?," is it satisfying or even possible to describe our efforts? Maybe yes. "What do you do in a writing workshop anyway?"

I started thinking that I should share the tingle and tension of arranging words only with a few chosen friends. Right away, I decided not to say anything to my mother when she asked about my activities, because she was uncomfortable with parts of my 2001 Finland trip report. I wanted to spare her the worry that my pen might be moving in her direction.

Maybe a few prepared sentences about the practice of writing would be useful and nourishing to respond to inquiries. "Thinking on paper helps make order of my thoughts and feelings." Or "My current writing aims to describe and reflect on my years as an architect and a manager," followed by "What do you think might interest readers?"

A couple of times, workshop members and friends informally asked if I were writing the thousand words a day, as I had so boldly set out to do. I reported yes, followed by the total number of words. Their supportive admiration helped keep my disciplined routine locked in. It was so rewarding to churn boxes of saved projects and records into pages of facts, decisions, and feelings arranged by date, subject, or idea. Now, 34 post-it notes stick to my bulletin board, with topics on them like the joy of architecture, working for large organizations, creativity in government, and my major architectural projects or managerial assignments by name. In my "memoir folder" sit 15 subfolders containing 111 documents of over 77,000 words.

It took years for me to find this merging point of readiness in attitude and availability of calendar space. Attending the workshop, Wednesday after Wednesday, held me to the task of plowing my piles of paper and photos into rows of readable building components. The next step will be to develop the themes, design my concept, calculate the dimensions, choose my voice and tone, engineer the structure, estimate the time available, and then start building—the book.

WHY I WRITE

Susan Antolin

A FEW YEARS AGO my husband, Ed, told me after work one evening that the sister of an acquaintance of ours had been diagnosed with advanced breast cancer and that she was told she would have only a year or two to live. We had met this woman and her family only once, but had felt a connection to her since her two children and our older two are the same age, which at the time of the diagnosis was two and four years old. Along with shock and sadness, I felt a sudden and overwhelming hope that this woman was writing.

I hoped that she had a written record of her thoughts so that her children would have more to cherish than photographs and stories told secondhand. I pulled out my own journal a bit more often and wrote a little extra around that time. The morbid thought plagued me for a while that if I were to die then, my children were too young to have lasting memories of me.

We lost touch with this acquaintance and thus never heard how her sister did with the disease. But I have often thought of her and felt a renewed energy for writing down the things I know would otherwise be lost if I didn't. I write my journal in a series of cheap spiral notebooks, and the current one is usually on the kitchen counter among my paper clutter, always close at hand. I write of the wonder and beauty of having children, and I write of the disappointments, jealousies, frustrations, and sadness right along with it. I want my children to read it all when they are ready to have children of their own so that they will be reminded that life with kids is not a smooth road.

Since moving to the suburbs five years ago I have been invited countless times to scrapbooking parties, where women gather to assemble albums of family photographs under the guidance of a consultant who sells the pricey products required to put the albums together. I declined the invitations at first and then finally gave in as these events seemed my only chance to get out and socialize with other mothers. I now have a carefully decorated scrapbook which the kids love to look at. There are times, though, when I look at it and wonder at the gaping emptiness of it as a means for passing on our family stories. All of our smiling faces hide the truth. Our lives are so much more than the pictures could possibly convey. After these events, I return to my journal with renewed energy.

Now that I am in this writing workshop, I am taking a tentative step toward writing for an audience broader than just my own family. It is scary and it is exciting. I now carry a little notebook in my purse and write in it at red lights, in grocery store parking lots, in my quiet garage after I pull in with my sleeping two-year-old buckled in behind me. I have another notebook next to my bed. I sometimes grope for it in the night and take it into the bathroom, where I jot down the thoughts that swirl in my head in the night. I have started writing poems, something I never imagined I would even attempt. The feeling I get after writing a piece I am proud of is euphoric. I want to slap someone high five. I used to look forward to an evening glass of wine, which I often had while cooking dinner. It helped me cope with the chaos of tired kids wanting more attention than I could give. The other day I noticed that we had no wine in the house and hadn't had any for over a month. I added it to my shopping list and wondered how I had failed to notice being out of wine for so long. I know this has something to do with writing. I am finding fulfillment and peace with words stirring in my mind.

From the class journal.

LEAVE OF SUBSTANCE

Nancy Deutsch

"I QUIT." "PLEASE ACCEPT my resignation." "Yo! Boss from Hell, I am outta here!"

I recite these phrases daily, even though I quit my job as a social worker two months ago. It's just that the exhilarating part was the quitting. The aftershock ain't so grand. As the Who warned us in *Tommy*, "I'm free, and freedom tastes of reality."

I can handle the issues that go with life in the recently-unemployed lane: the sleepless nights, the constant anxiety about income, the fact that I may never have health insurance again. It's the reactions I get that drive me crazy.

The worst one came from my psychologist neighbor. "How exactly are you spending your time?" she probed.

I had practiced several vague answers to deflect her interrogation, but once the stare of Freud's ghost was upon me I caved in. I sputtered like a car spinning its wheels in mud, splattering up the windshield of my life, dredging up every little project I might possibly pursue. I finally stopped to breathe and ended with a grand finale of ". . . and most important, I'm writing."

She was undeterred. "But that can't possibly be taking up all your time."

"How true," I continued. "Did I mention I'll also be working on a cure for cancer, going on a speaking tour for my new yet-unwritten novel, and squeezing in a couple of weekends with Mother Teresa?"

I seem to strike particular fear in the coronary-prone hearts of workaholics. We of the "no career identity" set must be their worst dreams incarnate. I have designed specific responses for their "What-are-you-going-to-do-with-the-rest-of-your-life?" Type A questions. If only I were brave enough to say them.

"Beats the heck outta me," I imagine myself saying with a stare as blank as my checking account. Or perhaps, "I plan to eat bonbons all day and then write a bestseller on dieting."

You'd think raising a child would help justify my unemployed existence. But I'm finding the added role of motherhood just elicits more anxiety-producing comments.

When I told my last boss I was quitting he said, "Oh, hmm, this is serious. Are you going to have another baby?" Apparently the only reason he could fathom any woman choosing to leave his dysfunctional work environment would be to procreate.

My dentist's reaction was equally disturbing. Between fillings (that I made sure I got taken care of while I still had dental insurance), I told him I quit my job.

"Oh, so now you'll have more time to spend with your son." He picked up a slender drilling object.

"Actually, I'm planning to spend more time writing, and I'll be doing some consulting," I mumbled through cotton-stuffed lips.

"It's such a great age to be with him. The time with your kids goes so fast."

Maybe he didn't hear me clearly.

Why was I so offended? I will have more time with my two-year-old son and I'm thrilled. It's the assumption that I can't possibly mean what I'm saying that bothers me. I've finally taken my life into my own hands, and my triumph is treated either as temporary insanity or as if I said I'm shopping for a burial plot. Both responses peel my fingernails from the thin ledge of courage I clutch.

It hasn't been a total drought in the support and encouragement division. Some people try to say the right thing, but their subtext gives them away. When I told a coworker I was quitting cold turkey she said, "Whoa, you're brave." Translation: "You must be out of your mind.

We're in the middle of one of the worst recessions in California history." My confidence took a plunge.

Bathing our son the other night, my partner Rich kindly offered a way out of my "Did-I-just-make-the-worst-mistake-of-my-life?" funk.

"Just enjoy the time," he suggested. "It ain't gonna last anyway."

Well, I am enjoying the time. In fact, with writing, child-rearing, and worrying there aren't nearly enough hours in the day.

Yesterday my friend Lisa left a message of solidarity on my answering machine. She said I was her new role model, and she plans to follow in my income-challenged footsteps as soon as possible. I suggested she get her dental work taken care of first.

Should Lisa or any of you out there decide to experience the agony and the ecstasy of telling your boss to take your job and shove it, I do have some advice to handle the mood swing that may follow:

1. Relabel the experience. You're not unemployed, you're taking a "Leave of Substance."

2. Call yourself a consultant. Everybody does it. For $20 you can get a business card to prove it.

3. Tell the truth. Say: "Things are going really well, I've never been busier."

4. Lie. Say: "Things are going really well, I've never been busier."

5. Chant daily: "My worth is not connected to my salary, my status, or my sanity." Repeat as needed, especially when filling out your tax returns.

I guarantee your self-esteem will improve within 30 working days. If not, let me know. However, it may take me a while to get back to you because things are going really well, I've never been busier.

HOW DO WE DO IT?

Kathleen Faraday & Robin Lawrence

ROBIN WRITES: "How do you and Kathleen write your column together?" friends have queried. Ours is the only column written with unblended voices and separate takes on the same idea that I have seen.

Double Talk and our style of working together have evolved. We search for an idea—an anecdote, scraps of conversation, feedback on specific columns, the season, holidays, rites of passage, life lessons, hard times—from a grab bag of inspiration.

Then off we go to "rooms of our own" to see if we can go with it. Kathleen often composes in her head as she flies around town; her room is her Explorer. I require a quiet space, usually at home, to see what shows up as I write.

Like jazz musicians improvising on the same melody, we practice and play together to harmonize our styles and points of view. The integrity of the column from beginning to end is our concern.

Before we had fax and e-mail, we met for coffee or a walk and exchanged first drafts. After reading them over, we would give each other feedback. Since we had done that with others in our writing group, this was a familiar and reliable process.

To work in tandem as we do requires trust and flexibility. With praise for the sentences we like and questions for those that are unclear or irrelevant, we fine-tune further. We decide who had the best opening and the best closing. Because of space limitations, it is like a puzzle to express ourselves concisely. We exchange second and final drafts and talk over further changes.

Lastly we decide on a title. Occasionally the *Sun* will exert editorial privilege and change our title for reasons of space—or so we've been told.

KATHLEEN ADDS: "What do you write about?" is a question often asked by friends out of town. "Oh, drivel" is my self-effacing response.

"Well, what kind of drivel?" the conversation continues, and I sum it up boldly: "Whatever happens to strike a chord as we metabolize life events."

And most of the chords that are struck are near and dear to our hearts. Friends overseas and on the East Coast follow the column on the Internet at hotcoco.com.

On Sunday, I nudged Robin in church and said, "Now there's a column," as the priest told of his Lenten restraint when a rude woman driving a Suburban while talking on her cell phone cut him off as she turned into Blockbuster.

Then to his surprise, there she was charging up and down the aisles still on the phone reading movie summaries to her kids on the other end. Amen!

Robin and I are similar in so many ways—medical backgrounds, involved with our families, love our gardens, enjoy cooking and sports, devoted to our pets. But don't ask us to write about the current political dramas. We might surprise you with our different views.

Column topics are a challenge, but often they find us. When Robin suggested this one—"how do we do it?"—my instant response was "by the seat of my pants."

Which reminds me that there have been a few ideas that Robin has vetoed—like the trials and tribulations of "the road warrior," the saga of the automatic airport toilet, which kept flushing the seat cover before I could sit down upon it!

You can see where my mind goes sometimes—right down the drain. So Robin reins me in and we get back on track.

Tuesday I read a column by Jolie Kanat about her address book. It took on a life of its own and immediately I wondered, "How come we didn't think of that?"

Life is like a real roller coaster ride with lots of "whoopees" and many stomach-grabbing "oh my Gods." Often we write about the highs and sometimes we choose the lows.

We are all on the same merry-go-round and being able to share experiences is part of the joy.

Appeared March 3, 1999 in Kathleen and Robin's column "Double Talk" in the *Contra Costa (CA) Sun.*

REBIRTH

Martha C. Slavin

I REMEMBER FLOWERS poking their heads out of the wet earth. My son Ted, at age two and a half, already knew the names of daffodils and tulips. We till the soil when the ground is just ripe for planting, not too muddy or too dry. The smell reminds me of dead cows, stretched out in the desert, dried up, ground up, tossed back to earth to begin life again. The hoe digs satisfactorily into the soil and pulls up great chunks of earth. I remember rolling out the clods still too wet to break up. I throw them into the bushes where they will dry up and disappear back down into the ground again. I remember springtime: coolness still in the air, the skies intense blue, close to the vernal equinox, the clouds gray and white across the sky. In California spring usually lasts for about a week and then it is summer already. This year we are tantalized by a day or two of bright, clear weather and then the rain comes again. Like all life, this season is sprinkled with touches of hope among clouds of doubt.

I started writing again after Ted was born. After six years, I have begun to wonder where my writing is going. Actually I always wonder that. I have also started reading other writers writing about their writing: Brenda Ueland, Natalie Goldberg, Anne Lamott, and Julia Cameron have all given me insights into the writer's life. Annie Dillard wrote of walking around a table stacked with piles of a manuscript as she sorts and changes and pulls out pages. I can't imagine when I will be doing that. What little I have written does not form stacks of a book.

I took this journal because I felt myself at a lull in my writing. I was too busy to spend too much time writing; nothing was coming out anyway. Now suddenly words are coming out of me in a flood. I've started essays and stories that I had forgotten were in me. The key, I found, was to sit down and say, "I remember."

From the class journal.

DREAM JOB

IN THE EARLY '70S, when I was just out of my teens and living in New York, the billboards appeared everywhere: "I got my job through the *New York Times*." A satisfied customer was smiling at the camera, the *Times* classified section in one hand and a mug of coffee in the other.

I was on unemployment at the time and aiming to secure two or three part-time, under-the-table positions to supplement my modest weekly dole. Usually I found my jobs by word of mouth or in the *Village Voice*, and never through the *New York Times*, but these billboards had me convinced the *Times* was the only way to go.

One Sunday I was studying the *Times* classifieds—perhaps imagining my own satisfied face on a subway billboard—when I spotted an ad in the editorial section. The hours were right, and I called the number listed.

A Mr. Franklin answered, an older gent. He was writing his memoirs and was in need of an editorial assistant. We agreed to a meeting that very afternoon.

I made my way to East 93rd and Lexington Avenue, near Gimbel's, a part of town I rarely frequented. Mr. Franklin's building was in the middle of a quiet block. I rang the bell, and he buzzed me into the lobby.

His ground-floor apartment faced the street and was just steps away from the building entrance. The door opened, as expected, but something seemed off. Then I realized that the apartment was completely dark, a black hole—I couldn't even see if anyone was inside. With adrenaline coursing, heart racing, hopes sinking, I prepared for my worst New York nightmare to begin.

Suddenly a light snapped on, and I saw a frail white-haired man in his eighties—Mr. Franklin. He was blind. I entered the apartment.

Mr. Franklin was solicitous, which helped allay my initial fright. Expertly navigating the clutter of his small abode, he offered me a seat, the straight-back oak chair next to his big messy oak desk, and sat opposite me, in the apartment's other chair. He described the job— standard manuscript stuff, except that I would serve as his eyes. I expressed interest, and he hired me.

We quickly arrived at a workable routine. He would dictate several sentences at a time, perhaps even a paragraph, and as he spoke I would pound away on his clunky old Royal typewriter. Then I'd read back his new copy, and we'd edit: he might want to change a word, or move a phrase or sentence or paragraph. I'd re-read the results to him, and he'd dictate some more. So passed each of our three-hour sessions, during which we generally came up with three or four double-spaced pages.

I never did find out how large a chunk of his memoirs Mr. Franklin had completed prior to my tenure with him, but he and I spent a lot of time documenting a pivotal event in his life: the day he'd lost his eyesight some 27 years earlier.

By all appearances Mr. Franklin had adjusted to his life as a blind man. He even became a bit of an activist, having started an organization called the Go-Sees, which made and distributed white-tipped fiberglass canes meant to encourage mobility for the blind. Sometimes, in lieu of editorial duties, I was called upon to make my own contributions to the cause, gluing the cane segments together, typing and mailing invoices, shipping the canes themselves, updating membership rolls.

I was paid a small hourly wage three times a week, at the conclusion of each of our sessions. Mr. Franklin would take out his wallet and unhesitatingly hand me my salary in cash—always the correct bills.

On my next visit, we'd invariably return to the day he became blind. Back then, when he was a sighted man, he lived on a large semirural property in Pennsylvania. One afternoon he was preparing to dynamite a sizable rocky outcrop on the property; he'd handled this kind of job before. But that day something went terribly wrong. The explosion took his sight. He was 55.

It was a sunny day, Mr. Franklin recalled; the sky was cloudless and brilliant blue. Absolutely nothing amiss—until the explosion. The blue of the sky was seared into every fiber of his being—it was the last sky he ever saw—and he was determined to convey it perfectly on paper. He wanted the sequence of events to make sense to his future readers, but mostly, I think, to himself. Each time I read back the paragraph or two of description leading up to the blast, he would fiddle with a detail here or there. He relived those horrific moments with a purely focused awareness as we combed over them for new kernels of truth.

In our several months together, we did not produce a finished manuscript. We didn't cover many topics at all—not his family, not his former profession. We didn't even complete the definitive account of his shattering accident. He wasn't surprised when I announced my plans to leave: I was about to move to California. I left Mr. Franklin grappling with his memories, while I went off to chase my dreams.

PLEASURES

SEIZE THE MOMENT

Anne Ziebur

ALL MY LIFE I HAVE COURTED this magical trick, this spur-of-the-moment decision to embrace whatever comes now, whatever suggests change and newness. The last painting on the living room easel would not exist today had I not followed my inner silent and wordless voice that said: "I want to paint. I want to paint right now."

Instead of paying the stack of bills or doing the stack of dishes, I leisurely set up the kitchen island, covered it with the paint-stained cloth, aligned the tubes of color, the pots with water, and the towels.

A close family friend had died the day before after a long and tragic illness. My painting of sea and shore, with one lone boat, sails filled with air under the wind-blown clouds, became a journey of companionship to one who was traveling her last journey known to us.

Barely a few days later, Shauna, 6, and Lindsey, 4, arrived like a celebration of new life for one of their frequent weekends at Grandma's house, my house.

After hugs and a kiss hello, they charged in with glee, brown hair flowing, as if they owned the place, wheeling their carry-on luggage behind them, wheels rumbling on the slate entry floor. They owned not only the place but they owned me. From the beginning to the end of the weekend I was completely theirs.

They knew of course that this was Grandma's house and that Grandma made the rules, but their time with me was their time alone, not anyone else's. They also knew that one of the fun things about Grandma's house was that sometimes we broke the rules. Having breakfast for dinner and dinner for breakfast was usually a hit.

Maybe a stranger walking into the house would also think the children owned it. Dollhouse, farmhouse, books on the low table, teddy bears everywhere, other stuffed creatures, a playhouse and a slide, beach balls, blankets, dress-up clothes, a kitchen drawer all their own, a chest with art supplies they could reach themselves, and in my room, their private collection of favorite videos.

Between the play, the meals, the comings and goings, our days were gone before we knew. Transitions took up a lot of time, whether it was setting up a meal or an activity, or getting ready to go out.

On Saturday we had a busy day, driving Shauna to a birthday party and shopping with Lindsey for cookie sprinkles and for clothes. Dinner had been late, and afterwards they went straight to my room where they nested on my bed among all the flannels and pillows. I loved to see them there, comfortable and snug, wavy brown hair against the pastel sheets. They were watching a short after-dinner video. Soon it would be bedtime, much later that night than other nights.

After doing the dishes, I sat down for a break on the low, wooden kitchen stool. I was unwinding when suddenly Shauna came running out of my room, jumped on my lap and hugged me. I loved the surprise, and kept her close as we wrapped our arms around each other.

"Grandma." Uh-oh, here it comes, the request I didn't expect. What would it be this time? Her soft skin and rich hair smelled sweet. "Grandma." She did her preamble just fine. "I know it's a little late for this," she said, "but could I, please, I really want to, could I please paint right now?" Inside me a part bigger than my heart and bigger than my brain had already said "Yes." But I pretended to think hard. "Well," I said, drawing it out while she spied my face, "well," and then exclaimed, "Yeah!" She cheered with me.

We brought out the bottles of tempera and filled the hollows of her round palette with each color. I got water and brushes while she put on her flowered smock and chose her paper. Quickly into her work, she asked me to join her. I set up my own supplies and we were both busily painting when Lindsey came running out of my room in her nightgown, brown eyes sparkling and her wide grin showing the dimple on her cheek.

"I want to paint too, I love to paint!" she cried out.

The atmosphere and the activity took on their own momentum, we were transformed into an exhilarated trio, doing something radical and unheard of, against the rules: staying up way past bedtime, painting late into the night. Of her painting, a small female figure whose mass of black hair was surrounded by explosions of red, Shauna said: "This is a Chinese Lady, as anyone can see. All around her are fireworks. This artwork is for Mommy and Daddy." Taking her painting in both hands, Lindsey brought it over to me. With a proud and impish smile she said: "This is for you, Grandma." A green slope studded with trees, a red church roof in back: she had painted the view from my living room window.

We had seized the moment. It was Saturday night at Grandma's house.

WHY I SWIM

Elizabeth Fishel

THE OTHER DAY WHEN I CAME HOME from the pool, glowing and singing to myself, my husband admitted that he has occasionally wondered if I'm having an affair—I always return from swimming in such a good mood.

Swimming is, indeed, much more than exercise for me—a passion, a mood-elevator, a daily meditation. The mindless, repetitive laps and deep, rhythmic breathing relax my chattering mind and center me the way staring at a candle flame calms a meditator. When I get to the pool my head is dizzy with daily dross and family concerns. What to make for dinner, how to counsel my sons, when to visit far-flung relatives, where to go for vacation? An hour later, my swim complete, I feel calmed and empowered; decisions have been made, perspective gained. Endorphins pour through me like an elixir.

I started swimming regularly before I became a mother, but though harder to arrange, it became even more necessary after my children were born. Then I discovered that swimming complemented and improved every phase of motherhood. When I was pregnant and feeling increasingly whalelike on land, the pool made me feel weightless. Soon the pool became my solitary escape as a weary nursing mother. Sometimes I'd persuade my husband to sit poolside holding our infant Nate in his arms. I'd nurse the baby and then duck into the water, depleted; by the time I emerged, Nate would be ready to feed again, and

I would be magically revitalized by my water therapy and once more ready to nurture him.

Sometimes during those first years, after what seemed like an endless day of childcare with no sitter in sight, I'd plead with a friend to bring her toddler to the pool, and we'd take turns swimming laps and watching each other's kids. When the boys were preschoolers, I'd round up a poolside teenager to look after them for a few dollars, then plunk them all down with popsicles and swim feverishly until the treats had melted and they wanted my attention again.

Now that they're school-age, they can even accompany me, and sometimes do, madly racing each other across the pool, while I swim my steady, motherly laps. But my sons remain more land animals— soccer, baseball, and basketball players—than water babies, and swimming thankfully remains a place to be alone. The flickers of guilt I've occasionally felt for leaving them to take a swim are snuffed out by the knowledge that I'm able to be a better, happier, and calmer mother when I return to them.

The pool is the one place in my life that is just for me. When I enter the water, I sink deep into another world, removed from the demands of time and space. Serene and turquoise, hushed, safe, enclosed, and womblike. Light shimmers through the water like darting fish. Every day a baptism, says a fellow swimmer, every day, a mini-retreat. When I'm there, I'm blissfully unreachable—can't answer a phone, drive a carpool, find a lost homework, rustle up a snack. It's a perfect antidote to the pressures of working, the dailiness of children's needs.

Despite their number one place in my life, I sustain my devotion to my boys by taking a daily breather. So no matter how much pressures crowd in on me, I'm religious about finding the hour it takes for a swim. Even if I'm not in the mood I still push myself to go, for if I don't swim, I'm crabbier, shorter-fused. Swimming provides the decompression between my two lives, gives me that personal oasis before I return to my loved ones. And it provides a vital message to my children: that their mom takes care of herself in order to care for them.

I've read that the best fit for a lifelong sport is one that matches your temperament. Swimming is that for me, contemplative, meditative, sweat-free; it's the one sport that can be accomplished lying down! So when my husband wonders if I'm having an affair, perhaps he's on to something. Like a romantic rendezvous, swimming is private and a change from my rushed routine. It's a time in the day that's just for me.

Appeared May 2002 in *Child* magazine.

20 WAYS TO SUSTAIN MYSELF
ON CRAZY DAYS

Ann Lipson

1. I DRINK LOTS AND LOTS OF TEA, herbal and black. Sometimes I prepare for myself an entire pot in our cast-iron teapot from Paris, but only when I am close to a bathroom. Tea, pee, tea, pee, tea, pee. I also like fat-free cocoa, especially on mornings faced with tasks I can't even bear to think about.

2. I stretch really tall on my toes with fingers grasping for the ceiling. That way I feel elongated, thin and light—almost floating away from the problems of grounded earth. I also like the reverse, reaching down to touch my toes, to reassure myself that I am flexible and supple, a reed in the wind, able to withstand the storms and squalls thrown at me. Then I like to dance to the pulse of music letting the rhythm and the beat dictate the steps.

3. I knit, taking care to have several projects going at once. I can pick up the easy project in stocking stitch, knit one row; purl the next, when I need to talk a family member through a heartache on the phone. I choose a complicated fisherman's weave when I need to concentrate and banish the world. Crimson mohair yarn perks up my spirits, while soft muted creamy alpaca wool calms my frazzled nerves, and multicolored angora, weaving all the shades of a forest on a summer day, feels like diving into a field of dandelion fluff.

4. I take long hot bubble baths with copious bubbles, aromatic candles, incense, and often a cup of tea or glass of red wine. I often take the latest *New Yorker* into the tub with me, and try not to get it wet.

5. Waking up early and doing the following ritual in this specific order puts a positive shape on my day, without which I feel befuddled and untidy, as if my seams are not straight, or I've misplaced something crucial: a) Read poetry, meditative or spiritual thoughts; b) write in my journal; c) prepare a "to do" list on a post-it, that I can then transfer into my Day Timer; d) read philosophy, biography, French or Spanish, or some of each depending how many minutes I can squeeze in at my desk, illuminated by a Tiffany lamp, bought by my husband who "gets it." All of this must take place before the siren call of the day's demands becomes unbearable.

6. I like to listen to music, all kinds, and introduce color into my life wherever and whenever I can. I write legal briefs listening to Bach and Mendelssohn; I bathe to Dvořák, and shimmy around the kitchen in my apron to the Rolling Stones. Color comes in flowers, fruits, and vegetables arranged in baskets, purple ink, ash rose soaps, my cranberry IMac.

7. Cleaning out closets, drawers, cabinets, and files is one of life's most satisfying experiences. To create order out of chaos comes as close to feeling godly as it gets. Achieving control of my stuff puffs up my "I can do" quotient for a week. Tossing out clothes I haven't worn in years confirms and solidifies the edges of my current identity and somehow sharpens the focus of my life. It is a declaration: this is who I am after all.

8. I like to sort and arrange photos into albums and decide which ones I want to enlarge and which ones should go to the grandmas. Five minutes into the task, I am so lost in memory and the love of the smiling faces frozen in time that my heart opens up a mile wide.

9. When my psyche starts to squeeze and contract, then I know it is time for a walk. The more the constriction and sense of impending doom or suffocating claustrophobia I feel, the longer I like to walk. One summer, in the throes of severe emotional pain, I used to walk seven miles a day. The pain was more manageable that way and I lost some pounds as an added bonus as well as breathing the freshest air imaginable.

10. Reading French never fails to delight me, while listening to spoken

French reinforces my French self, a self I like very much, and in which it is very pleasant to reside. My French self is charming, noted for her lack of ego drive with a definite predilection toward all that I consider to be amongst life's highest goods—love and cultivation of conversation for its own sake, the human connection above all else, a fixation with the shopping, preparation, and eating of finely prepared tasty food, and an engagement with a level of discourse that challenges all of my faculties. My French self is more alert than my American self, and to the extent I want to be on my toes, the French will bring that out in me. To the extent I want to find an alternative to all that is bruising my spirits, the French language never fails.

11. Caring for my plants satisfies the nurturer in me. Watching them blossom and grow in response to my mindful fertilizing and watering feels like a connection to life itself. On a really bad day repotting a plant can be as satisfying as finding the perfect preschool for a child. I have every faith that the plant or child will thrive in the new environment.

12. Simply focusing on breathing can calm a racing mind. "Remember to breathe" was the mantra of one of my work colleagues once when, under pressure, I would forget, and turn shades of blue and gray. Breathing slows down the thoughts, and brings me, imperfectly, back into my body.

13. I like to call a friend, preferably someone like my friend Rina, with whom a conversation never ends, and is only broken up by the demands of living in the real world. When I call there is no need for small talk. We get right down to the latest metaphysical or emotional knot where both the pleasure and the solace come from peeling away the layers of meaning. Eventually we arrive at the nub of a problem, and cherish the emotional closeness between us that ensues, whether we solve the problem or not.

14. Remembering to set my table with the colorful ceramic or glass pots we have purchased in Italy and elsewhere in Europe elevates aesthetics to a prominent place in the day-to-day art of living. When the fax that just came in sets my mind boiling, remembering to use a special cup and saucer from Lucca, Italy, or the south of France, gives a concrete jolt to my head—I have another life; this problem is only a part of the whole, not the whole.

15. When I am really wounded by the world, there is no better remedy than staying in bed until noon with a pile of books I am reading at the moment, with pen and paper. After several hours of keeping company with the voices in my books—either characters of fiction or biographers—I am ready to get up and face the world again.

16. Has nothing changed since Cleopatra's day? Not for me when it comes to giving myself a manicure or a pedicure. It is the ultimate luxury to indulge myself with new products and an uninterrupted hour in the bathroom to add elegance and color to my self-presentation, soothing pressure to aching feet and flagging self-esteem.

17. I like to clean. When deadlines start to inch forward like pouncing dragons, I have the cleanest house imaginable. That is just the time when polishing a sink with Ajax can unlock the key that has been delaying a project, or dusting some gleaming oak can reflect back not only my image, but also the key to fixing the problem.

18. When I want to really connect with a fellow human being, my grown-up daughter in Santa Cruz has got to be first. I, like everyone else around her, love to spend hours sharing life's problems with her, although I don't let on that that is the reason for my phone call.

19. I like to eat cottage cheese in mini portions throughout the day. Cottage cheese for me is the perfect food, primarily because it is comprised of protein, but just as importantly, I really like its taste, its blandness, its compatibility with grains of raisin bran or cheerios to create the ultimate treat.

20. I like to stop and listen to the wind rustling in the trees. The sound comforts and excites at the same time. It lets me know at night that I am alive. The sound comforts the cradle of my bed.

DO YOU HEAR WHAT I HEAR?

Ines Swaney

IT WAS STRANGELY COMFORTING to read in a recent article in the *San Francisco Chronicle* what I had suspected all along: accents can really steer you in strange directions.

Apparently some students at UC Berkeley had been wondering what their instructor was referring to when he mentioned an "auto-Italian" type of government. They finally came to realize that what their foreign-born teacher had really said was "authoritarian government."

This brought me back to my early days at Cal. As a newly arrived freshman, a foreign student, I had to plunge into listening to classroom instruction where all subjects were taught in the English language, a situation I had never experienced in my native Venezuela. Now in math class I kept hearing the lecturer say something that sounded like "time," which would make me glance at my left wrist, but my watch revealed nothing special. Then I realized the word was "times," which really meant "multiplied by."

Whereas some people suffer "double vision," I have diagnosed myself as a carrier of the "double hearing" syndrome. You can almost be assured that if something can be heard in more than one way, thus presenting more than one meaning, I will hear it. Perhaps I've developed this condition as a kind of malpractice insurance: my regular work as an interpreter between the English and Spanish languages, in either direction, takes me to conferences, court appearances, law offices, business meetings, and jail visits, among other places. I'm required to quickly comprehend what someone has just said, and instantly render it, with identical meaning, into the other language. And I don't always have a chance to double-check and verify what the original speaker has just said.

Not only is English a challenge when listened to by foreign ears, but nonnative speakers of the English language can sometimes innocently lead you along a path of misunderstanding.

A few years ago, my European-born Aunt Agnes was visiting us at the time when most back-to-school purchases are made. When I was considering buying some shoes for my daughter, Aunt Agnes politely advised me to look out for the sickness of the shoe. I started having thoughts of other people who may have been at the store earlier, trying on that same pair. Maybe they suffered from athlete's foot or some other ailment? Then she showed me an example of what she meant: "Look here, a nice and sick shoe." I then realized that what she really meant was "thick." For some strange reason, the following day I walked past an establishment that had a sign up front: "Shoe Clinic." Of course it makes sense, I thought: a clinic is where you go when you are sick, as shoes sometimes are. More recently, over the phone, I was puzzled over my aunt's use of the surname "Harris" several times during our conversation, until I realized that she was describing some internal conflicts taking place in Canada, and that her statements to me contained the word "harass."

In the midst of the "Costco grazing diet," when you pretend that the edible samples you savor at the warehouse store will add up to a cheap meal, I heard a uniformed lady claim that the samples she was in charge of distributing were "pat pree." This utterance required just a slight mental conversion on my part: she meant "fat free." But then a few days later, I witnessed an honest misunderstanding when I overheard that two people failed to meet at a prearranged place, because one of them went to the "copy shop" while the other had gone to the "coffee shop" instead.

What started out with my initial frustration as a college student attempting to absorb classroom instruction spoken in English has now turned into a lifelong habit of collecting sound bites that appear to have double meanings, or that are challenging to decipher. The nature of my work is such that every day I may be faced with a different topic or specialty. When I first heard a scientist from Scotland Yard testify that "in the laboratory we use hydrogen peroxide to sterilize cats," I had no idea that a few moments later he would be clarifying this with an explanation—"I mean, sterilize cuts, such as when you cut yourself"—while proceeding to demonstrate with a slashing motion from his right hand over his outstretched left finger.

Why would a classical radio station, with no commercial interruptions, suddenly be talking about "Taco Bell"? "Oh. I see... they meant the Canon by Pachelbel!" I had just turned on the radio, at the end of the sentence. Shortly thereafter, another announcer seemed to be identifying an upcoming piece as "Variations on the theme of Tequila . . . " which turned out to be *To Kill a Mockingbird*.

What I had once thought was a strange hobby of mine—the collection of all these unusual things that I happen to hear—has now received its official blessing and validation thanks to an article in the *San Francisco Chronicle*. I look forward to expanding my ever-growing collection.

SENIOR MOMENTS

Ellen Hauptli

AT FIRST BASE, MY TEAMMATE Marylou can cleanly scoop those pesky throws in the dirt, or stretch the extra inches to nab a short throw to make the out. At bat, she can place the ball where she wants: often over the first baseman's head, and when the fielders have shifted to the right, she sends the ball screaming down the third-base line. Marylou is eight years older than me—58—the oldest person on our co-rec softball team. I admire her tremendously for her skill on the field but just as much for continuing to play into the discount age. Marylou has watched me slowly improve my skills since joining the team eight years ago. She's been patiently waiting for me to grow up so I could join her senior women's softball team, the Silver Streaks. I am finally old enough to appreciate what a blast it is to play ball with women of a certain age!

I am the rookie at 50, just old enough for senior tournaments. At least half our players are in their sixties. I had finally begun to feel like an adult, comfortable with my own version of modern maturity, but now I have been thrown back into a state of apprenticeship again. I get advice from my older teammates about how to make the energy last through three games in a row, how to harmonize and work with the team, and what is expected of me as a courtesy base runner. In this league, if there is a batter with defective knees who can get on base, she is allowed a proxy runner for the rest of the dash toward home plate. Also, to help save knees and other body parts, we field five in the outfield instead of the standard four, and sliding is always forbidden at home plate—the runner runs off to the side to a second home plate. She has to make it there before the ball reaches the catcher at the one in the batter's box.

Senior women often play in a regular local league, but also travel to exotic places like Palm Springs, Reno, Tucson, and Sunnyvale to participate in weekend tournaments. A few Septembers ago, for instance, we competed in Denver. With some hard line drives and a few double plays, we qualified for the 1999 National Senior Games—the Senior Olympics—in Orlando! A teammate or two might compete in other events as well: 68-year-old Janet will throw horseshoes, 64-year-old Reno is still a competitive sprinter, and 61-year-old Cherrie ran hurdles in the '64 Olympics in Tokyo. Reruns in Orlando?

A tournament means high excitement and hard work. My first senior softball event felt more like hardball. I flew to Burbank, rented a car, and then drove two and a quarter hours to Palm Springs where we played in 95-degree desert heat. Of course there was a hotel involved. Imagine my surprise at being given the AARP discount. The 25-year-old behind the desk didn't even ask to see my I.D. My husband lamented later, "Oh, Ellen, they're making you a senior before your time!" Competing in a senior league has to do with age, yes, but disposable income as well: I figure each of the hour-and-a-quarter games in Palm Springs cost me about $58, excluding meals, beers, and ibuprofen.

After playing three games on Saturday and well into our second of three games on Sunday, my body began to exhibit many of the senior signs: a hobbling Walter Brennan gait to and from the field, difficulty negotiating the stairs, moaning while bending over to tie my cleats, and the worst—short-term memory loss. How many outs did we have? What inning was it? Where was my position? Oh, where was my ginkgo biloba?

But how refreshing it felt to be among ladies who did not moan and groan about the size of their tummies, their cottage-cheese thighs, or their crepey wattles. Nor did they comment about other people's. We did, however, make occasional disparaging remarks about the lack of aged skin on some other teams' members: "Let's check her I.D. Those don't look like 50-year-old knees."

Supportive chatter flourished in the dugout and on the field: "Hey girl, great snag you made!" or "Don't sweat it, hon. Now you've seen the way she hits, you'll get it next time" and "I'll back you up!" Thank goodness in this league it's no disgrace to openly admire the skills of the opposing team. When a play is well executed, we say so. Ever hear Barry Bonds do that? In the fifth inning, if one team is ahead by 15 runs or more, the ump will mercifully end the game. My son who plays Little League calls this the slaughter rule, but in our league perhaps it should be dubbed the euthanasia regulation.

My mother came to watch us play in the Sunnyvale tournament. She sat in the stands with her camera and hot dog, adding to my sense of adolescence revisited. My teammates made a fuss over her, but after a while they tried to recruit her for the team. Imagine a mother-daughter combo at the Senior Olympics.

My first copy of *Line Drive* senior softball magazine arrived last month. It's the "Official 'Senior Softball World Series' Publication." As I flipped through, I scanned articles about various men's and women's teams around the country, batting strategies, and an article entitled "Sex and Softball: Go for It." Yes, the controversy about sex before a big game is discussed by senior players, too. The general opinion about sex is the same as it is about playing softball—do it whenever you possibly can. And how well the advertisements in this newsletter targeted senior ball players: hotels, vision and eyeglass businesses, and funeral homes—for that last big OUT.

This last year, my team split in two so we could play in both the 50- and 60-plus age brackets. There are brackets going up to 80-plus, so I expect the Silver Streaks will be in business a long time. Marylou opted to play with us young'uns because, as she put it, "I'm on the *cutting age*." But I'd say that's where every one of us is.

THE FABRIC OF OUR LIVES

Kathleen Faraday & Robin Lawrence

KATHLEEN WRITES: Have you ever loved a dress beyond its place in your wardrobe?

If I asked my girls what dress they would most associate with me, I think the vote would be unanimous—the red lace dress.

For many years, I never gave it a thought. Then, one summer while on home leave from overseas, I discovered that my mother had created a wonderful room for the grandchildren and filled the closet with all of our old party dresses. It was a treasure trove for dressing up and make-believe.

There was one dress in particular that my girls and their cousins fought over—the red lace one. It had a fitted bodice with a red satin lining, a full skirt that twirled, and spaghetti straps studded with rhinestones. The dress has been immortalized in many a photograph capturing the imps teetering on high heels in feigned *Vogue* model stance.

I wore that dress to my first prom. I was a sophomore at Uniondale High School on Long Island, going to the junior prom with my high school sweetheart, Henry. I can still hear my dad teasing me with "I love Henry, I love Henry."

For many years, the traditional prom photo occupied a prime place on my dresser.

When dress-up days were over, the dress again went back into obscurity. Then one day, a moving van pulled up to our house in Lafayette with my piano, all my dolls, and the old party dresses. My mother had finally moved from the big house after my father died. And there it was, the red dress.

In 1994, it came alive again in a play in Berkeley. In 1995, the phone rang and I heard a voice from the past. Henry was going to be in town and hoped to see me. My girls were all a-twitter. He was barely in the front door when my girls coaxed me into putting on the dress. I was very smug about being able to zip it up all by myself! Now I didn't say I could breathe, but I did endure long enough for a reunion photo to tuck under a magnet on the fridge.

I come by my nostalgia naturally. The red dress is tucked away now, but I am certain that it will be worn with glee by my step-grandmunchkins as well as my own grandchildren, when they grace the planet. And someday, many years from now, someone will say: "Do you remember Mom's red lace dress?"

ROBIN REFLECTS: If I could choose one garment from my childhood that I will always remember, it would be my mother's blue kimono. It was made of finely woven cotton, midnight blue with a pattern of white abstract figures both astronomical and Japanese.

The sleeves were especially beautiful: bell-like, they were wider on the arm than at the shoulder. They hung in folds unless the arms were raised, which then revealed their shape and the contrasting white facing.

The kimono had a presence of its own—elegant, mysterious. Mom wore it in the evening after the household had settled—we children with homework or TV, my father often joining in to watch and editorialize on the TV program. She seemed to float from room to room, sometimes with a purpose, other times as if she were somewhere else.

I knew that the kimono was from Honolulu. My parents met there in the course of their first jobs teaching at Punahou, just after World War II. She was a humorous, lighthearted pianist and he, a handsome, ambitious coach. They were both from the mainland. My father, who grew up with the rigors of Midwestern weather, thought he was in paradise. Photos from that time show them on the beach—Dad in a Hawaiian shirt, Mom with a lei around her neck. Sometimes they would reminisce about sunsets they enjoyed under the banyan tree on the beach in front of the Royal Hawaiian hotel to the plaintive verses of the song "Blue Moon." Now I wonder if the kimono took my mother away from her cares and back to the islands.

When I was in college, my mother offered the kimono to me to wear in the dorm. She said she hadn't worn it after she and my father separated. I tried it on just to see how it felt—light and airy. But at the same time, I was uneasy, so I returned it to my mother. It was so reminiscent of her at a happier time.

Several years later, my mother died unexpectedly. In the course of gathering and sorting her things, I came across the kimono tucked in the closet. It was clear that she had not worn it in some time because a fine layer of dust lay upon the shoulders. After a long, hard look at the lovely kimono, I put it on the pile of clothes for Goodwill. Today, I wonder where it is and if it casts a spell for someone else.

Appeared June 18, 1997 in Kathleen and Robin's column "Double Talk" in the *Contra Costa (CA) Sun*.

SUMMER VACATION

Kathleen Faraday

AS I PASSED ONE GLORIOUS FIELD of sunflowers after another, I looked out over the countryside and had to pinch myself to believe that I was actually on vacation doing something I had dreamed of—biking through Tuscany. Pedaling up one hill and barely down another before it went up again, I remembered the first words of our guide in his delicious French accent. "Flat is boring," he declared as he described our nine days of biking.

As I pedaled past a field of sunflowers with drooping heads, I identified with them immediately and asked one of my companions to stop and take a photo of me in their midst—only my yellow bike helmet gave me away. I blessed each shade tree along the way, as we plotted the distance between trees in 90-degree heat for a water break. Fortunately I teamed up with Coleen, a cardiologist, whose presence provided a certain level of security should I just simply croak. Her husband did the extended routes with my super biker friend Jim. They applauded our determination to complete the basic 30- to 40-mile routes without van support, dubbing us "Team Sunflower."

Back Roads Bicycle Trips do a marvelous job, but I had to ask myself which letter in the word hills didn't I grasp. The brochure mentioned the *hills* of Tuscany, walled *hillside* cities, lovely hotels perched on *hilltops*—and how did I think I would get there? I switched from one low gear to another, refusing to use my "granny gear" until

I simply couldn't push the pedals around one more time. I finally named my quads Meg and Myrtle in overheated delirium so that I could have personal conversations with them in between chanting my mantra, "Push, push, mamma mia, push." Someone said, "It sounds like you are giving birth."

"Dead right," I responded. "I am giving birth to my new self!"

As I pedaled up to the walled city of San Gimignano, I thought about its famous historical torture museum. Perhaps I would offer myself up as a wax model on a Back Roads Bike for the Year 2001 display!

The trip was a challenge, but I loved knowing I made it each day and nothing could match the pleasure of collapsing into a chaise by a glorious pool overlooking (of course overlooking—we were on a hill!) the absolutely beautiful countryside. Not to mention the elegant meals and my freedom to eat it all because I would burn it off the next day.

Four days of relaxing in Umbria at the home of a dear friend and daily hikes up to a medieval church—on a hill—were marvelous preparation for the bike trip. Just sitting in the grass watching the bees in the clover as we contemplated life in general qualified as vacation from day one. Time in Florence and Rome after the bike trip was exhilarating, but already I missed my bike. Would I go again? In a heartbeat.

ARGENTINO

Terri Hinte

MARCOS AND MARINHA, MY HOSTS in the emerald city of Belo Horizonte, were taking me to a Christmas party. It was a perfect summer evening, the last night of my stay in the mountainous Brazilian state of Minas Gerais, and I had caught the holiday spirit.

As we arrived at the Passarinhos', where festivities were getting underway, I felt the gears in my brain start grinding in preparation for social chatter. My Portuguese served me well enough one-on-one but tended to stall when required to produce quick banter in large groups. Marinha was my safe harbor while I sized up this gathering.

I found the refreshments and helped myself to a cold *chopinho*, then walked outside for some air. Typically, the Passarinhos' house was enclosed by a high solid wall that afforded security and privacy from the street. Partygoers were thus mingling in the front and side yards, the sultry air perfumed by jasmine, the flamboyant trees in flagrant scarlet bloom.

Strings of tiny lights illuminated the yard as darkness finally fell and the music rose from background to main event. The irresistible sounds of samba brought a number of people to their feet, and started mine itching as I sat sipping my beer. It wasn't long before I was invited to dance, by an ardent bear of a man named Tadeu. He was sweaty and sour-smelling and a bit drunk, but I was quite thrilled to be up and moving with the crowd. Tadeu, in fact, was dancing by himself,

off in his own sensory world, and so, therefore, was I. But that was fine
with me. In a fundamental way, I had traveled eight thousand miles to
be doing exactly this, seeking some kind of intimate knowledge of the
samba, with the body as hierophant and the soul the ecstatic recipient
of its gifts.

While conversing with the rhythms on the dance floor in the
vicinity of the frenetic Tadeu, I scanned the yard, savoring the styles of
the dancing couples. One man in particular was making the samba all
his own with movements of wonderful finesse and a captivating swing
(or *sue-wing-ghee*, in the local parlance). As soon as the record was
over, I bade Tadeu adeus with a thank-you-man and wasted no time in
approaching the evening's prize dancer.

"*Quer dançar?*" I proposed, a bit breathless with anticipation.

"*Lógico,*" he smiled, taking my hand. But of course!

His right hand alighted on my blue-draped hip, my left on his
shoulder; our remaining hands found each other high in the air, laced
loosely, as hips and legs and feet began to respond in unison to the
tensile rhythms. It was simple, and sublime.

We introduced ourselves not long into our maiden dance—his name
was Argentino, a handsome man of mocha complexion, slender build,
and uncommon grace. He described himself as a poet. I was Teresa the
americana, as usual the only one present and therefore charged with the
burden of explaining Ronald Reagan. But Argentino offered instant
expiation; like everyone I'd met in Brazil, he brightened at the mention
of San Francisco, my home base, and offered the requisite compliments
on my Portuguese ("*Você fala muito bem!*").

Frankly, though, talking got in the way of the purity of the dance.
We were a team now. As each record ended, we remained poised for
the next, grinning, relishing our glorious calibration.

Doubtless there are men in the world who love to dance and are
good at it and who can lead a woman partner through an experience
where two are one and aren't even thinking about taking off their
clothes. I had just never met such a man. Dancing with men meant
dancing near them or at them, as with Tadeu, or leading them, as with
my American friend Jim, who could expertly follow my every step and
spin.

But here with Argentino, it wasn't even a matter of his leading me; it was more like his moves *were* my moves, we were just making them together at precisely the same moment. Moreover, his *sue-wing-ghee* was of a piece with mine—closer to the pulse of the music, right *in* it rather than spurting out from it. Peripherally I could see many such gushing dancers in the yard, exhausting themselves after one go-round. Argentino and I, we kept percolating, marveling at the persuasiveness of a hip with intent, exploring the rich dimensions of movement in the smallest possible space. We *were* the heartbeat of samba.

How many hours passed? We hadn't left each other's company all evening, nor had the smiles left our faces. But the music had quieted down, the party was rapidly thinning out, *madrugada* was settling in. Marinha and Marcos were saying their goodbyes to the Passarinhos, and that meant I would have to bid farewell to Argentino.

We faced each other with this task, still aglow. "*Você dança como um anjo*," I said helplessly. You angel you.

Not missing a beat: "*Aprendi esta noite contigo*," he replied, the picture of serenity. I learned tonight with you.

In English the concept of speaking *with* someone is self-evident, but in Portuguese you also learn with someone, not from them, and you dream with someone, not about them, suggesting that these are not solitary activities. Clearly Argentino and I had both dreamed of a mutual surrender to the music on a tropical Christmas night. As we danced together, we learned how to make our dreams come true.

"Argentino" was the first piece Terri wrote in class. It won first prize at the 1995 Book Passage Travel Writers' Conference writing contest and was published in *Travelers' Tales Brazil* (1997).

DOWN THE COLORADO:
A SOUL JOURNEY

Lorna C. Mason

I SEEMED TO BE at the bottom of the world. Huddled against the scorching sun in a curve of red river sand under a blue beach umbrella, I was writing in my journal. The date was June 5, 1995. Above me rose a cliff of black lava, which radiated and intensified the 100-degree heat. Above it was the intensely blue sky, broken now and then by jet trails. A few feet from my sandy seat was the smooth-running, deep-green Colorado River. About 50 yards downstream the great river dropped 37 feet—almost four stories—in an imposing cascade of roaring, white foam. This was Lava Falls, the largest and most respected rapid in the Grand Canyon.

I was part of a group of 16 traveling with Grand Canyon Dories, which had been an independent operation but was now owned by OARS, a California-based business. Dories are small, oar-powered, wooden river boats. On a previous trip I had traveled part of the river on a raft, and it was then that I heard dory boatmen referred to as the "princes" of the river. Most people descend the Colorado River in rubber rafts, some of them huge motorized pontoons. The major advantage of rafts over dories is that they can bounce off rocks. The four-passenger dories are more maneuverable, and much more fun, but rocks and boulders offer them no forgiveness. Therefore dory boatmen must be highly competent.

The river skills of our crew made the trip safe; their human qualities helped make the trip memorable. All of our boatmen had gone beyond any "river rat" stage that might have been part of their youth. They were all 30-something—mature and accomplished individuals.

From Jano Kempster, our one female guide, I learned that female guides consider themselves "boatmen." When she wasn't on the river, Jano, in camp, always wore a full skirt—the envy of those of us who had never imagined a skirt would have its place on a river trip. But Jano knew what she was doing. The skirt was cool protection against the late afternoon sun.

The leader of our expedition was Andre Potochnik, a geologist. With his rugged good looks, including a dark moustache, Andre was the epitome of the healthy outdoorsman who gave us geology lessons using only a stick in wet sand.

A third boatman was red-bearded Roger Dale—"Jolly Roger," I thought of him. One day when the river was higher than it had been in years and had collected all kinds of flotsam, Roger showed adeptness in pulling into eddies of flotsam and extracting unopened beer cans.

Black-bearded and Scottish-born, Dugald Bremner, a professional photographer, was the fourth boatman. I hold a special fondness for Dugald because he was particularly attentive to me. On all our hikes I was a laggard, but Dugald, who had the agility of a goat, often stayed with me. Plodding along at my slower pace, we told each other our life stories, and he shared his vast knowledge of the plants along our way.

Dugald was also very interested in the human history of the Grand Canyon. I felt my age, but also impressed him with my stories of going through Glen Canyon in 1957, before Glen Canyon Dam submerged that beautiful place in 1964 and created Lake Powell. Before Glen Canyon Dam, the Colorado was warm and red, but now the river originates from the bottom of the dam and emerges clear and cold.

On one of our hikes up a side canyon, I was ready to stop at the first lovely watering hole we came to, but Dugald urged me on, helping me scramble over the boulders on the path. At last we came into one of the canyon's sacred places—a round enclosure with a spring slashing down into a shallow pool below. A canopy of trees provided shade. Flowers and ferns were abundant. We sat for a time on sandstone slabs and savored the coolness and greenness. Dugald had brought along a book of Terry Tempest Williams, a Utah writer, and read aloud a story in which Williams described her mother finding a mass in her abdomen but then delaying a trip to the doctor so that she could go down the Colorado, where she found such peace.

Our party of four dories and two support rafts had taken 12 days to reach Lava Falls since embarking at Lees Ferry 179 miles upstream. The leisurely pace had allowed whole days for exploring side canyons and, even more important, allowing time and quiet to experience awe. Wherever one is in the Grand Canyon, there is something awesome—waterfalls emerging from high cliffs, the bloom of a red cactus flower in the hollow of a boulder, sandstone stained and carved in such a way as to evoke Georgia O'Keeffe's intensely organic images, mossy grottoes, rock art carved by Anasazi Indians many centuries ago.

The geology of the canyon itself is like astronomy—almost incomprehensible by our time scale. The river has cut through more than five thousand feet of rock to the continent's very bedrock, formed almost a billion years ago. The canyon is the result of a great uplift of land—the Colorado Plateau. While the land was rising, the river kept cutting through the strata. It includes red sandstone, yellowish limestone, gray shales full of ancient marine skeletons, and the shiny black basalt of the inner gorge—the deepest part of the canyon. For most of our journey we could no more see to the rim of the canyon than could the tourists at their outlooks see the river below. One needed to be a bird, or in a plane, to see the great steps of colorful eroded formations that stretched up and away from river to rim. In one side canyon Andre pointed out the Great Unconformity, a place where Vishnu schist, which is about 1.7 billion years old, is overlayered by the Tapeats sandstone, which is 550 million years old. Missing between is about 1.3 billion years of earth history. How many mountains had formed in that time? How many rivers and seas washed them away to leave no trace? It was mind-boggling.

For a year I had dreamed of taking this trip, for I was recovering from aggressive and debilitating treatment for breast cancer. My dreams were full of rivers, and I longed to take a river trip for the sake of my soul. I was seeking to accept my life as part of the great rhythm of Mother Nature and to find peace in that acceptance. Now for 12 days

I had exulted in this journey. I treasured the "sacred places," where drips of water created chapels of living green. I also adored the thrill of running rapids. It was pure joy when I could ride cowboy style sitting on the very prow of the dory and yelling "yahoo!" as the boat reared high over a wave and then slipped down over it. It was soul-soothing to drift down quiet water, looking for ducks in the reeds or scanning the cliffs for mountain sheep. I could understand why Terry Tempest Williams's mother had wanted one more trip down the canyon before entering the nether world of illness and even death.

From the beginning of the journey the guides had spoken with some concern about Lava Falls. Always a challenge, the rapid had been changed by a flash flood that spring. None of our guides had seen the new rapid. So now I sat on the right bank while they scouted that side, which used to have a chute that carried boats through. No longer. A huge boulder arid "hole" blocked the chute. A hole is a low place in the river through which there is no current. Boats can get trapped in holes.

We hoped for better luck on the other side and rowed across. From the flood debris on the left side of the river, Roger and Andre selected tree-sized logs and threw them into the rushing river. From the bottom of the falls Jano and Dugald watched their exit from the rapid. We might make it down a chute on the left side, they decided, but it would be tricky. It would be necessary to enter the rapid at just the right point to avoid both boulders and holes.

Finally the word came: it was go. Andre and his passengers pushed off first. It was a tense time as we stood on the bank to watch him aim at the big tongue of waves that could provide a safe ride. The passengers helped, throwing their weight toward side waves to help keep the boat steady. In just a matter of seconds Andre was through.

I was in Jano's boat that day. As did the others, we prepared for the run by putting on the flip lines. These are lines that wrap round the boat so there is something to hold onto if it flips. For the first time on the journey I had worrisome thoughts for my personal safety. What if we flipped? Was I strong enough to survive the rapid, even with the help of a life jacket? This was not some commercial water-thrill ride. This was real, and death by drowning is a recognized—but small—risk of running the canyon.

We pulled out into the current. The water was smooth. Ahead a crest of white water marked the point where the river dropped out of sight. Steadily Jano pulled toward the tongue of waves on the left. I rode in the bow with a hefty young man. There was a still moment like at the top of a roller coaster, and then we were in the midst of white water pounding us from every direction. My bow partner and I leaned into side waves, yelling with exhilaration. We too were through in seconds and then, because the boat was full of water, bailed like crazy.

All the boats ran Lava Falls without incident. We pulled into the beach below the rapid and euphorically toasted our success with champagne. In his toast, my partner in the ride said he wished his mother were like me.

Lava Falls is the last of the really big rapids on the Colorado. The next day I would be leaving the river, flying out by helicopter. The thought saddened me, for the river had become holy, and the canyon itself a holy, comforting place. The pace of river time, in which one can only go as fast or as slow as the river, was as nourishing as the opportunities to be exuberant or reflective. There was a lot of raucous silliness that night at the entertainment called "Lava Follies," but I wasn't feeling very silly. Instead I read aloud my journal entry of that day:

It takes you deep into time and yourself,
this river that flows through Earth's history.
Here powerful currents sculpt out canyons;
here gentle drips nourish mosses, ferns, and flowers,
bringing green life to the arid landscape.
The river speaks in thunders and booms, splashes and gurgles.
The tinkles and murmurs of side canyons become hymns to Mother Earth.

The river gives freely of itself.
Sand and wetness cling to us like a second skin.
In the peace of quiet stretches, in the exuberance of white water,
in the timelessness of sand becoming rock and rock becoming sand,
I find happiness.

It bursts forth as whoops of delight and as quiet awe.

On this journey I have been nurtured by good comrades
and by boatmen sensitive, knowledgeable, and skillful.
I leave the river tomorrow, but it has poured into my soul,
leaving me sated with feelings of love, health, and joy.

FAMILY TALES

THE INTERIOR STORY

Michelle Wells Grant

I STAND IN THE DOORWAY of my parents' bedroom and peer in. It is a bit like peeking into a schoolchild's shoebox diorama. I see the interior story.

I am still not accustomed to the look of this room, although it has been three years since it was redecorated. It seems so very different to me, such a departure from the way it looked for ten years. Amazing how one can take a room, just a box really, decorate it with paper, paint, and pieces of cloth, and alter it so drastically.

I am used to the previous colors, rich and deep, in keeping with the rest of the house. I remember the caramel-colored grasscloth on the walls and the jewel tones of the Oriental carpet repeated in the fabrics of the room. I always thought that my mother, who has wonderful taste in decorating and a keen eye for design, should have been an interior designer or architect. Instead she spent her life helping others heal through her work as a physical therapist.

The redecorated bedroom is different from her usual style; charming but different. It is so bright and cheery. The walls are painted lemon-yellow. The fabrics, five different rose prints that are all compatible, create a garden-like room drenched in golden sunlight. Plump pillow shams recline on the rose-dappled bed. Yards of rose-print fabric swag gracefully at the window, and the round bedside table wears a rose-patterned skirt. On one wall hangs my great-grandmother's

colorful quilt; a fan pattern on a buttercup-yellow background. My
mother loves that quilt because many of the pieces are scraps from her
own childhood dresses. Another visitor to this house would find the
bedroom engagingly cheerful and inviting, but I know the room is so
planned, so deliberately cheery. I know what happened in this room to
prompt its transformation. I know why this bedroom needed changing.

Three years ago, and for just three months, my parents moved their
bed out of their own bedroom and moved a hospital bed in. My 43-
year-old brother, Mark, had become a quadriplegic as a result of a car
accident just four months earlier. He had never married and had no
other family to care for him. No nursing home would take him because
his condition was so complicated. Mark would be the new inhabitant of
the bedroom. My parents, who were retired and in their seventies,
would now sleep in the den.

The cherrywood dresser, which my parents bought soon after Mark
was born, was half emptied of its contents to accommodate my
brother's few belongings. Carefully arranged framed photos, my
mother's jewelry box, and pretty accessories were swept off the dresser
top and replaced by countless prescription bottles, inhalers, lotions, and
ointments. The hospital bed, which was a formidable stainless-steel
structure, loomed heartlessly in the room. A motorized wheelchair was
parked in the corner.

The room became a nucleus for activity. Day nurses, physical
therapists, social workers, and even paramedics raced to Mark's bedside
on several occasions, when he stopped breathing or lost consciousness.
People came and went all day, yet no one assisted Mark more than my
parents, who were always at his side: feeding him, turning him, bathing
him, brushing his teeth, changing the television channel. At night Mark
called out to my mother for a drink of water or medicine. She rarely
slept.

Then one day after lunch, Mark died. He was strapped into his
wheelchair in the living room, looking through some family photo
albums with my father, when he had what appeared to be an aneurysm.
My father said Mark was looking backward at his life, at old yellowed
pictures of us as kids at the beach, then of us as toddlers holding Easter
baskets, then of us as babies in our playpens. I like to think he just kept

going all the way back to the very beginning and beyond.

This had been my parents' bedroom for ten years, but the three months with my brother had spoiled the room, tainted it, given it a different aura, instilled a memory that twisted the heart and caught in the throat. It had to be changed, transformed, made unrecognizable.

My mother painstakingly peeled away the tragedy and painted over the memory. She scraped and washed and spackled the walls. She sanded them and primed them. She sewed drapery, pillow shams, and a bedskirt. The project took weeks, but she would not let my father help. The walls must be as smooth as a baby's tender cheek. The linens must be fresh and new. Only she could do it.

I step further into the bedroom, the pretty little diorama. It is only a box, after all, redecorated and well appointed, which contains a deep interior story. The past is peeled and scraped away, the future is painted cheery and bright. The pain is covered. The room is void of Mark. The rest of us are represented here, on the dresser or the yellow walls: my father's World War II photo, he's young and handsome in his Navy uniform; my mother's bronzed baby shoe, my grandmother's brass lamp; my daughter's portrait and her framed artwork; and, of course, the heirloom quilt. My sister and I loom big as life in a photo portrait hung over the dresser. But Mark is gone. So deliberately. I see him only in the roses in the fabrics. He loved roses. I wonder if my mother chose the fabrics with this in mind, that there might be yet some trace of him here. The image of her tossing red roses into the ocean at his memorial service hangs in the air.

From this perspective I see another layer of the story. I see the scars gouged deep into the walls, that no amount of sanding or lemon-yellow paint could hide. The bedroom was where he spent the last three months of his life, tragic as they were. But his demise, his accident and quadriplegia, was not the most devastating part of his life. The great tragedy was his whole life, which he had lived with schizophrenia; alone, confused, and scared. It was the whole life that had been torture; the accident was simply the means to exit the life.

My mother knew this. She painted the walls lemon-yellow to camouflage the face of pain in a room where her son had suffered through the last three months of his life. But it wasn't the last three months; it was the whole 43 years. It was his life. It was a mother's anguish and bewilderment, guilt and frustration over why her son must bear such unhappiness, why he was denied an ordinary life. Was it something she had done? Was it something she could have prevented? Could she have made it easier for him? She had, after all, given him the life.

I move to the bed and sink into the softness of the comforter, a bed of roses. I am completely inside the diorama now, seeing it from all sides. From this perspective it is still a pretty little box, sweet as a child's school project. But from here, I clearly see the third tier of the interior story. The ceiling lifts and the lemon-yellow walls fall away like cardboard, to reveal the infinite landscape, the true interior story. My mother's story.

MY MOTHER'S BATH

Joan Stevenson

I KNOW AT THE DOOR even though I know my mother is waiting for me. She has already turned on the water for her shower so we will not have to wait for it to be warm. Her big concern is that giving her help with the shower will inconvenience me. I tease her that I am evening the score for all the baths she gave me. She has lived nearby in the retirement home for five years. Her caregiver is on vacation and I am filling her role for two weeks.

It is difficult for my mother to be naked in front of me. We were a very private family and at first, I, too, was uncomfortable, but as I help her I am aware of her body. She surprises me with a comment: "I'm glad my man isn't around to see this old body." My father died over 30 years ago.

Awkwardly, cautiously, she steps into the shower; she cannot scrub her back because of her limited range of motion. I tell her I can't do that myself. She loves the rubbing and I am once again reminded of how little physical touch older people have with others.

I try not to show I am apprehensive, terrified she might slip on my watch. She finishes and I help her dry off. I rub lotion all over her very dry skin, and I comment on the fact that at almost 93, she has gorgeous legs. She blushes but I know she is pleased.

It is a privilege that I have been asked to bathe my mother. For most of my adult life a continent and many months separated us. At 88,

Mother chose to leave her home in New York and move across the country to this retirement home near me and my family. It was amazing to watch. She viewed the sale of her old house with delight, making sure it was shown in the best possible light. She treated prospective buyers like guests and with those she particularly liked shared special secrets about the house.

A month before the sale was final, I flew back to help with the packing. When I inquired what furniture she would be taking, she looked me in the eye and replied, "I have lived with these things for 60 years. I want all new." And so it was that she put on a heavy winter coat, pulled her knitted cap over her ears, and walked out of a house full of the past into a blustery winter evening. She never looked back.

In the years since, I have held her hand through four hospital stays and two major surgeries. I admire her grit. I watched her learn to walk with a new hip and heard her recite the instructions of the physical therapist. "Butt in, chest out."

I observe how carefully she lives her life. Everything is in order. A list of birthdays and anniversaries sits on the kitchen counter. I keep her in cards and stamps. Obscure cousins I have not seen in decades are remembered. Bills are paid as soon as they arrive and bank statements are balanced. The calendar dictates her life. The menu for the week is posted by the day. Her clothes are laid out each morning and the bed made before 7:30. Breakfast consists of cereal five days a week, frozen pancakes on Saturday, and frozen waffles on Sunday.

Each time I knock on my mother's door I am reminded of the gift I have been given. Not only all these years as my mother and my friend, but she has also been a model for me—warm, upbeat, and resilient. A life lived with courage and grace.

Appeared September 2002 in *Boomers' LifeStyle* magazine.

A U-TURN ON MEMORY LANE

Mary-Jo Murphy

WHEN MY MOTHER REMEMBERS, all the past is inspirational, magical, and unrecognizable to those who lived it. In her retelling, events become far better than the originals. My four sisters and I roll our eyes to heaven. "Give us strength," we pray silently, "to live through yet another rendition."

Vacations and holiday stories are especially suspect and undergo the most dramatic transformations. Our Christmas tree was always stunning, selected carefully. One Christmas, my dad, unable to find a full enough specimen, bought two scrawny pines and tied them together. The tree was always decorated with care and to perfection. I remember, heedless of decorating etiquette, gleefully tossing handfuls of silver spaghetti, until the tinsel hung in unsightly clumps.

Midnight Mass reviews found us peaceful and inspired. The silent night was always clear and bright. It usually snowed. The truth was, snow was rare. Daddy often overdid the Christmas cheer and missed church altogether. "Never. Your father always went to church with me." That's what she remembers.

Mother's childhood holidays were chaotic, so ours were enchanted. According to her, we all patiently took turns opening presents that were "just what we wanted." Taking turns required much more patience than I had. I longed to rip open packages willy-nilly. And, I have learned with my own children, some begged-for item was always missing. Was she truly unable to keep track of the details of the past or embarrassed and disappointed by what reality did to her best intentions?

Subjected during the year to Mother's endless shopping expeditions, Daddy procrastinated. On Christmas Eve, an hour before the stores closed, size ceased to be an issue. Color and the general appeal of the item were his criteria. Her face registered various negative emotions as she opened present after present of oversized clothing and personal items. This particularly annoyed her, because she liked to show off her curvaceous figure, but didn't want to be considered fat. Daddy would return the objectionable items. Eventually he switched to no-fault toiletries. He has been dead for over a decade, and Mother still hasn't used up the Jean Naté after-bath he presented her every year.

Events were reshaped so as to be unrecognizable. Arguments were interesting discussions. Adolescent rebellion always ended in heart-to-heart sharing. Was it because her own childhood deserved reshaping? Given up at three months old, just before the outbreak of World War I, she spent her early years in the New York City Foundling Home. Transported on the historic Orphan Trains, at around two years she was adopted in Wyoming. When she was five her parents returned to Connecticut, hiding her origins. She discovered her secret at age 18, but at her mother's request kept her father unaware. She struggled with her loyalties, and up until a few years ago, when we sisters initiated the search, had made only a half-hearted attempt to put the puzzle of her first years together.

Her adoptive mother, a manic-depressive, was in and out of a mental institution. I spent three months in residence at that same facility as a nursing student. Only then did Mother tell me of the pain and loneliness of those years. Perhaps her storytelling was not so much bravery and optimism as an attempt to make sense of the mixed messages that were her life.

Reacting to the mutability of her truth, when I retell a story, I watch my children's faces. Their command of details far surpasses mine. Most adults have long since lost the discrimination that unclouded, perceptive youth takes for granted.

Reality, however dismal, is authentic and what I choose to tell. As a mother I have an intense passion to remember "the way it really was."

My commitment to truth is absolute, but at times unsettling or even mortifying. An embarrassing event my sons are willing to retell could use Mother's touch. The original and therefore true version happened this way:

Their father was back in the city working and I was alone with our sons at our vacation home near Lake Tahoe. We are prone to sunburns, so I was in a rush to get to the beach before midday. Neither cooperated. The morning was sweltering and the boys were in an immovable summertime state.

"One more minute, Mom. I really want to see this" came a reply from my older child, watching yet another cartoon rerun.

"Can we eat something before we leave?" said my youngest, sitting down to begin a drawing. They felt no urgency. An hour and several unheeded suggestions later, I felt hopelessly trapped.

"We'll be here all day, coloring, eating, watching TV," I said. Now, I may value the truth, but I have lots of other faults and slamming doors used to be one. Frustrated, I stormed downstairs and let go my wrath on the door. Determined to calm myself, I took a few deep breaths, splashed cold water on my face, and put on my bathing suit. More composed, I grabbed a towel and headed for the door, confident that now I could act more adult and command their respect and attention. I even imagined them apologizing for their behavior. The door wouldn't budge.

What had I done? I am still not sure how my temper tantrum forced the door past the frame to dislodge a nail that made the door unopenable from the inside. Now, I not only felt trapped, I was.

My sons played, unaware of my captivity. "Guys," I called, trying to sound dignified, "are you there? Mom needs your help." Suddenly, the TV, games, and eating forgotten, they hurried to stand outside the door. "I've. . . um. . . locked myself in," I said, feeling altogether as stupid as I deserved to feel. I explained how easily they could extricate me with a hammer. "Just bang in the nail that's in the way, because Mommy can't open the door." Silence.

"Should we let her out?" they asked each other between giggles. Their decision wasn't an easy one. They did. We went to the beach. Years later, it still brings smiles to their faces and a blush to mine. But it's true in the telling.

When my own childhood memories surface, they need to be verified. But milestones are difficult to substantiate, because from my mother's point of view memories should be happy, therefore alterable. Something as awful as my slammed door anecdote would likely be blocked from future consciousness. My mother retained only the bits of reality that made a satisfying story. So her daughters' personal events were interchangeable. My ordeals could, in retelling, belong to any one of my four sisters. My growing pains were suddenly theirs, their best friends mine, all experiences improved in the retelling.

Many exciting trips to New York City ended by us getting lost on the way home. My theory is that my father hated to leave so much that his subconscious kept him driving in circles, over the wrong bridges. For years I thought Connecticut was an eight-hour drive from the city. According to Mother, her husband could get anywhere in Manhattan. In her version the lost part is totally forgotten.

"It reminds me of our trip to Washington, DC in your Volkswagen," my youngest sister begins. I finish her sentence: ". . . where I drove and kept getting lost, and it was sweltering, and Daddy would say, 'Go this way.' And Mother would say, 'Are you sure? I wouldn't. . .' and there I was in the middle of an intersection, with everyone beeping at me. . ." We grimace at the unpleasant authenticity.

Memories can't be changed, and I've come to believe they shouldn't be. I won't revise the past. I'm a realist. Mother's mis-rememberings compel my sisters and me to rehash in an attempt to seek our own clarity. We've found that reality, the clear unadorned pathos behind the slammed door, is where the fun is.

CORNUCOPIA OF CLUTTER

Michelle Wells Grant

IN A CRAZY, MIXED-UP WAY, I am thankful for the very things that cause me grief. I am thankful for the bounty of our daily clutter, the feast of messes, the abundant chaos of my household. But it is not my own clutter, nor is it my husband's belongings strewn hither and yon that I find noteworthy. Adult clutter is dull and unamusing. It is the cornucopia of "kid clutter," generated by our eight-year-old daughter Elizabeth, which spills color and flavor into our lives, along with woe and aggravation.

I come across the remnants of Elizabeth's creative play and the products of her zany imagination, and somehow take comfort in it. It is the half-finished puzzle on the coffee table, kittens in paint cans, that makes me feel her in the room when she is absent. It is the bulletin board plastered with her artwork; the colored pencils, chewing gum wrappers, and rock collection stuffed between the cushions of the sofa; the blue acrylic paint smudges on the kitchen cabinet knobs that tell me where those little hands have been. It is the abandoned bologna sandwich with only one crescent-shaped bite taken from it, long forgotten after pals call her out to play. It is the smell of her funny hamster in its stinky cage. It is the dining room table heaped with the latest school project; a shoebox and some clay and purple scraps of felt. Or the colony of Barbie dolls residing on the living room floor, in all their accessorized glory. It is the sofa cushions, which seem to leap to the floor of that room on cue the instant Elizabeth enters it. I gripe when I find these things, even curse, and I would be thankful if they were picked up and put away. Clearly this is a plan to sabotage my efforts to keep a tidy house, and I swear she intentionally leaves these inexplicable calling cards behind to insure my insanity. But way down deep I cherish them. They are the signs and symbols that say a kid lives in our house, and not just any kid, but the treasure who is mine.

I discover melted chocolate on my dryer. I find a wad of bubble gum in the toilet bowl and the dog's leather leash hooked up to the toilet paper holder, no dog tethered at the other end. The soap dish is filled to the brim with water and the mushy bar of soap is floating on the surface like a dead fish. I notice Elizabeth's beloved Honey Bear, a six-inch threadbare teddy bear who has been with her since Day One, peering at me beseechingly from inside the window of the Easy Bake oven. I rescue him and comfort him, tweak his worn felt nose and rub his shiny black eyes until they twinkle again, then hold him to my face and smell him. Smell her.

It is this bounty of weird things in strange places that I am strangely thankful for; these goofy, quirky remnants my child leaves in her playful wake, like a trail of special bread crumbs that only she could scatter. These things that make no sense to me but perfect sense to her, in her racing, soaring, imaginative mind. They make me stop a moment and think of her, my one and only child, my greatest gift and blessing, and somehow, her messes become forgivable. While I gripe that I hate to find them, I would hate more not to.

The memory of a somewhat orderly house before Elizabeth was born is vague and colorless; neat stacks of magazines on end tables and sofa pillows nicely plumped. Perhaps there was a necktie tossed over a chair or cartons of Chinese take-out abandoned on the kitchen table, an empty Coke can here, some junk mail scattered there. But by comparison, I realize now I did not know the meaning of the word "clutter." There were no games and puzzles jumbled in with the organized books on the shelves, no backpack or bicycle helmet flung across the polished dining room table, no green spots drawn on our miniature Dachshund's smooth red coat in magic marker, no Elmer's glue bottle glued to the kitchen table. No telltale signs of mischief or creative play. No pulse, no life, no visual feast, no reason by comparison. No reason to be thankful. No fun.

I have a lot to be thankful for—a good husband, my comfortable house, our health, my lucky, lucky life. But in a crazy, mixed-up way, and for all my incessant rantings for order, I am thankful for these vestiges of my child's play and antics, the fallout of her presence in our lives and the ever-present traces of her precious, fleeting childhood. When I enter our living room and find a tiny Barbie doll shirt hanging from the finial of my Tiffany lamp, stuck on by the sleeve like a miniature banner flying high, I mutter something unbecoming, then give thanks for the little hands that put them there.

SUNDAY IN THE BLACKBERRY BUSHES WITH REBECCA

Lori Rosenthal

SUNDAY AFTERNOONS FROM MID-JULY to early August mean only one thing in our Montclair household: blackberry-picking time! It has been this way since our kids were born ten and eight years ago. We have pictures of toddlers wading through the brambles trying to reach the purple candies resident in the trees. And we have pictures of children in strollers, holding containers of blackberries and eating in handfuls. The purple stain covering the lower half of their faces tells part of the story. The big smiles planted on their faces finish the tale. Yes, blackberry picking is a time we celebrate joyously in our house. And the celebration is currently underway.

And so it was this past Sunday when my eight-year-old daughter and I took off on our bicycles to reach distant berry patches (distant is such a relative word with an eight-year-old in tow). We rode from our modest height in the hills down Thornhill, a route heavily sprinkled with blackberry bushes. As always, we met other pickers and exchanged the normal blackberry picker's banter.

We start: "Sure are plentiful this year, must have been the heavy rains." They respond: "Yep."

The conversation continues in turn.

"What are you going to make with yours?"

"Oh, a cobbler or two, maybe a pie. What about yourselves?"

"We're jamming today. Blackberry jam is our favorite. Providing we get a big enough haul."

"Looks like you're well on your way."

"You too, happy picking!"

They might be right, that we are well on our way. Then again, they've never picked berries with Rebecca.

She's a good picker, all right. Can spot the purple ones from any angle in the bush. Knows the right level of tension to pull so that only the ripe ones come off the branch. Knows to avoid the ones close to the spider webs. Knows to hang on tight to her container, lest it fall accidentally and spill its contents. And definitely knows to avoid the berries on branches below her knees. That's dog territory. We like our berries pure.

And so we pick for a while. Not in silence. Never in silence with Rebecca. We talk about life. We talk about the sharp thorns. We talk about the spiders resident in the bushes. We bemoan the short lives of the insects they have captured. I listen as she blows on a spider or two to see if she can rouse them. She names each of them. She gives them personalities and occupations.

"You know, you're good company, Rebecca," I say.

"Thanks, mom" is her reply.

After a while, I notice that the rhythm of our picking has changed. I pick and she talks. After a longer while, I notice that it has changed again. I pick and she eats. One by one, five by five, handful by handful. The berries quickly disappear.

"Rebecca, I thought we were picking berries," I admonish.

"We were," she answers, "but now I'm eating."

"Well if you're eating, how will we get enough berries to make jam?" I ask.

"You'll pick enough," she responds. "I trust you, mom."

"Rebecca, why do I take you berry-picking with me?" I ask rhetorically.

"I lighten your load," she promptly responds. And flashes me a big smile as she plops another enormous, juicy berry into her mouth.

It is the same smile I've seen in the entire collection of berry-picking pictures. The purple-lipped, purple-toothed moment of joy that says summer is here and freshly picked blackberries make life worthwhile. In that instant, Rebecca reacquaints me with one of life's important lessons.

I reached for the plumpest, ripest berry I can find and plop it in my own mouth. There's no better time than a blackberry-picking Sunday to practice lightening my own load.

FOR SARA

Dian Gillmar

We sit on the end
of the dock,
my grown daughter
and I,

far away from the routine
of our lives,

the sun warm on our faces,
the lake gleaming before us.

We dangle our feet
in the cold water,
talk of nothing,

Yet everything that matters
is there for me
in her willowy presence.

She holds my past
lightly in the folds
of her being,

My love, my mistakes,
my longing for her happiness.

Suddenly we see her little son
running toward us,
with his bucket of stones to share.

He holds the bucket carefully
in front of him,
both hands on the handle.

We call out,
"Be careful, Jacob,
walk, don't run!"

And our moment passes
like the stone I throw
into the water, the ripples
going around and around

and out into the sun
as she gathers her son
into her arms.

VOICES

WHEN I THINK OF THE WOMEN who helped me become the woman I am, I hear voices, and I remember the occasions that prompted them to speak.

The woman who clearly formed much of what I am and whose critical, possessive voice I have tried to silence is my mother. I hear no words. I only know her being within me, the part of me that isn't as generous as I'd like, the perfectionist, the woman who hastens to form judgments without adequate reflection. As I've grown older I've learned to hear her other voice, the loving, caring, patient one, the voice that has made me resilient in times of difficulty and able to reach out with love and patience to my own children.

The voice from my girlhood that comforts me is my Aunt Lena's, my mother's older sister. I spent some of my summers as a girl on my uncle and aunt's wheat farm in eastern Colorado. I only have one clear memory of her words to me. The incident that prompted them appears to be of little significance, yet they were spoken in such a nurturing way as to stay with me. I'm standing at the ironing board in her sunny kitchen ironing my pink and gray plaid sundress. I am 12 or 13. The dress has a circular skirt, and as I struggle to place it on the board, she helps arrange it so the plaid rests at a diagonal and shows me how to iron it on the bias. Because she isn't critical, I can feel the satisfaction of ironing that skirt so that it will hang properly.

Whenever I think of that moment other memories of her come to me. Her laughter, the lightness of her step, her general demeanor of happiness and the pleasure of living. I remember helping her make noodles. They stuck to the counter when laid out to dry, because I had forgotten to put down wax paper. She laughed as we struggled to free them, not at me but at the struggle we were having together over a few noodles. It was uninhibited laughter, the kind I never experienced with my mother and in which I joined her.

I don't remember women teachers' voices growing up. The only woman professor I had at Brown was more man than woman. She taught psychology which at that time at Brown was based on Pavlov's theory of conditioned reflexes. We never touched on the richness of the unconscious nor the emotional complexities behind human behavior. Her name was Dr. Rosemary Purell, but we mocked her by nicknaming her "Posy."

I had two significant nurturing voices among the faculty, but they were men. The one woman's voice I did hear in college was Nancy Duke Lewis, dean of what was then Pembroke College. But I didn't hear it until the day before I graduated. She called me into her office to tell me two things: that I mustn't expect marriage to answer all the questions of my life and that I'd be happier if I would gain a little weight. I was to be married the day after graduation, and I was very thin! She was a maiden lady, a mathematician, quite feminine, and comfortably plump. I liked her, but her life didn't speak to mine at that point. It was only many years later that her words, "Don't expect marriage to answer all the questions of your life," took on significance. I've spent the last 40 years determining for myself the truth of her words.

Another voice I hear is my grandmother's. I had gone to visit her after I returned from a trip to meet my future in-laws. She lived alone in a small house next to my mother's younger sister. Her presence had always been a comfort to me for she seemed calm in contrast to her energetic and often frenetically active middle daughter, my mother. I told my grandmother that I didn't think that my future husband's mother liked me for she had suggested that I go home earlier than planned, saying that I must be homesick. I wasn't, but because she monopolized her son's attention I became angry and withdrew. My grandmother assured me that I didn't need to bother whether she did or didn't like me: the only bond of concern was between my husband and myself. My grandmother said that her relationship with her own mother-in-law was fraught with difficulty. Her candor in revealing something so personal was in great contrast to my mother who never shared her most personal feelings with me, and I never forgot the intimacy she created for us in that moment of sharing.

It is my mother's voice, however, that keeps coming back to me. Once she was sitting in my kitchen watching me prepare dinner for my daughter, her two friends from the East who were to be her attendants at her wedding the following day, and ourselves. I had returned the day before from a business trip and had met her plane the same evening. She said, "You are so remarkable. I could never do all you do." I felt her words came from a thought she had held for many years but had never shared until then.

She was 85 and had the beginnings of Parkinson's disease. I began to grieve for my eventual loss of her at that moment, and for the next two years of her life I thought from time to time of what she had given me. I realized that she expressed her love not in words so much as in actions. She celebrated my birthday every year that I was at home by baking an angel food cake which she decorated with pink roses. She made me birthday dresses, often embellished with embroidery or tucking, until I was old enough to express my own taste and then we shopped for the fabric and pattern together. After my husband left and I had to move, she came and packed everything for the movers while I rested in bed with a sprained back. She then unpacked everything after the move and helped me set up housekeeping in our new home. I was unable to speak of my grief at losing my marriage and the man I still loved, and to my immense relief she never asked for an explanation, although I'm sure her mother's heart grieved as much as mine.

A few weeks before she died she gave me the gift of her final words. She lay in a hospital bed barely able to speak and unable to swallow. She took my hand in hers and said, "My little girl, you have been through enough." I had been struggling for over five years to provide care for both her and my father. He had finally died the year before. She had never before acknowledged the magnitude of my task, and I was filled with an enormous sense of relief. I took her frail body in my arms, and she said, "I love you a bushel and a peck," quoting words from a song that had long been an affectionate expression between us. We knew we were saying "Good-bye."

She died two weeks later, a few days before Christmas. I was in Chicago with my daughters and their families when the nursing home called. Throughout the days and weeks of grieving I held in my heart her final words and knew I had been truly and well loved.

CRADLE AND ALL

Rebecca Kaminsky

OUR CULTURE CONSISTENTLY DARES US to be perfect mothers. "Choosy moms choose Jif," "Momma makes clothes bright as the sunshine" (Clorox)—advertising hammers in the message constantly. Up until the first time I had to take my son to the ER, these slogans and the accompanying cultural pressure were merely a source of irritation for me, something to arouse my "feminist ire" as my friends like to call it. My son Sam was four weeks old. I had planned to follow every possible child-rearing mantra that might improve his health and well-being—breast-feeding, organics, co-sleeping, no pacifier. This baby was going to be the most nurtured, loved being on the planet.

I ate perfectly during my pregnancy, leafy greens and whole grains until I threw up. After Sam was born, it took me a few weeks to get the hang of breast-feeding in public. To celebrate, my husband and I dressed up for our first dinner out with the baby. I was so excited—I finally fit into a pair of pre-pregnancy jeans—that I decided to jazz them up with my platform heel sandals. On our way out to the car I tripped, fell flat on my face, and Sam flew out of my arms right onto the pavement. My life was suddenly in horrifying movie slow-motion. I struggled to get my bearings and lurched over to where he was to pick him up. He was breathing, but he wasn't crying, just totally stunned and silent. My husband's first reaction was to bring him inside the house, that he would be fine, just a goose egg. But Sam's silence was too weird, too chilling. He remained that way all the way to the ER. I remember feeling horribly guilty beginning right at that moment. Just that afternoon I had been praying that he be quiet or asleep during our dinner, for just one night of peace. And now this. After a harrowing night—CAT scan, IV, and all—we found out that he'd fractured his skull. It sounded absolutely terrifying, but it is actually less serious than a concussion. The test results were good and our pediatrician informed us that unless he reinjured himself, he would be fine; he would probably just have a headache for a few days. But for months afterward I felt so excruciatingly guilty. I would replay the incident over and over in my mind—why was I wearing those shoes? How dare I, a mother after all, want to be sexy? How could I have wanted to go out and have fun? I should have been at home, breast-feeding in my husband's boxers and a nursing bra! Despite his doctor's reassurances, I didn't believe Sam was really OK until about a year later when he started to talk.

After the accident, I spent a lot of time trying to get a perspective on what had happened and how it might change my budding child-rearing philosophies. I realized that anxiety over Sam's safety and my abilities had been driving my zeal all along. I had wanted to find a theory to follow, an easy answer to a deeply complicated issue. As horrifying as the accident was, it forced me to wake up. I decided that the best I could do was to love my child and just dive in, do whatever worked without such a rigid game plan. I couldn't really control everything and my attempts to do so were taking away my joy and ability to live in the moment. If I wasn't having fun and feeling relaxed at least some of the time, what was the point of having children? I was always worrying about being perfect and having trouble just enjoying life, enjoying my son, my husband, my wonderful family.

Cultural pressure to be a perfect mother comes not only from advertising (where of course all the solutions can be bought) but also from parenting literature. That literature could be considered advertising as well, in order to sell books, parenting magazines, and the like; but in order not to fall prey to total cynicism, let's accept the premise that much of the literature actually aims to help parents as well as to sell books. It still doesn't matter what particular child-rearing tactic is being discussed—the pressure on the mother (yes, even in this day and age, it is still almost always the mother) to follow a particular theory or suffer the consequences is still always the same: breast-feed or give your child allergies, take out the pacifier or damage his teeth, put her to sleep in a crib and she'll be too independent and uncaring, let her sleep in the family bed and she'll live at home until age 45.

These messages remind me of scare tactics used to sell home alarm systems, except that they are used to sell a baby product or a parenting book. Where does this cultural pressure come from? The world is so fragile today (terrorists, snipers, kidnappings) that appealing to a mother's worst fears does sell, but I think there is a deeper message to be looked at. Something about keeping women—mothers—doing our jobs. We live with the best technology in the first of first-world countries, and still are told if X doesn't happen our children will suffer. Also, where is the outside help in this equation? Husbands, life partners, not to mention the village—why is keeping our children safe only a mother's responsibility? I was buying into the sexism that I was so aware of as a younger, independent woman—where was feminism to help me here?

Perhaps these cultural prohibitions aimed at mothers are so deep, feminism has had difficulty wrestling with them. I've certainly seen the staunchest of feminists (myself included) get obsessed over any one of them and take them to outrageous conclusions, blinded by worry over her child. I know one mother who won't allow so much as a drop of food not labeled "organic" to pass her two-year-old daughter's lips. Another was completely convinced that Indian food gave her breast-feeding child an upset stomach (her son had a particularly rough night of crying after she went out for a delicious curry dinner) so she swore off all Indian food until her baby was off the breast and eating solids. So many of these prohibitions, despite the grain of truth within them—organic foods only, no pacifiers ever, no weird foods while breast-feeding (cauliflower, cabbage, I've even heard chocolate)—seem to play the role superstition once played in our mothers' and grandmothers' lives. Growing up Jewish, I heard all the superstitions in my culture: tie a red ribbon on an especially attractive baby's toe to avoid the evil eye, spit three times if you mention something good, don't put a *kane ahora* (jinx) on something.

These things stick. I remember receiving a lovely red sleeper from a friend in the mail and dressing my son in it. After a day of particularly vigorous crying, I was convinced the red must have made him angry—read: it was "jinxed" (I was so sleep-deprived from night feedings he actually seemed to be growing devil horns)—and didn't dress him in red for at least a year. And Jewish culture certainly doesn't hold the monopoly on superstition. Who hasn't sung "Rock-a-Bye Baby" forgetting about the real words, the real consequences to the mother who puts her baby's cradle in a tree to let the wind do the work for a little while? We all want easy instructions for keeping our babies safe, when in the real world sometimes things happen that are unpreventable. That unpredictability can be so terrifying that it leaves us clinging to any theory that promises an easy answer.

Sometimes the best we can do is love ourselves, love our children, and try to stay flexible. Let them have candy once in a while, sleep them in the crib if we are too tired or in the bed if they (or we) need extra comfort, and meanwhile encourage the rest of the world to help us with this grave responsibility. Instead of worrying about every small detail, our precious time might be better spent pressuring publicly for things like flex time for the nonprimary caregiver, affordable childcare, and a little less onus on the mother, thank you very much.

I NEVER EXPECTED

Mary-Jo Murphy

THE LAST THING IN THE WORLD I ever expected was that I would become the mother of sons. During my single days, I had seriously wondered if the name Mom would ever be applied to me. Still, when I dreamed of my future life, I always imagined a sweet daughter, an improved version of myself. In fact, I had already named her, not realizing that her future father might have an opinion. I was sure she would be the best of me and everything I hadn't been. I never doubted her gender.

My own mother's dated notion that muscular development was "not feminine" would not encumber my daughter's athletic ability. With long hair that I could braid and fuss over, she would be the ballerina I would have become, except for my mother's prejudices and my incessant chattering during my lessons. She would be a runner, but she would discover her talents early.

And on a ski slope, she would be both graceful and strong. She would play the piano the way I would have if my parents had not given away our piano in frustration, because I practiced only on their sleep-in mornings. She would be an artist too. When she was older, we would shop, and then she would share the peak moments of her life with me over lunch. I would be her confidante. I would understand her, and she would be keenly in tune with me. We would be great friends.

"You're having a boy." The voice on the phone was giving me the results of my amniocentesis. A year and a half later I heard the same words, only this time "again" was added. My mouth said "wonderful," but my mind asked "why?" Why would a woman with four sisters and twelve cousins, only one of whom is male, a woman whose mothering images held only girls, have two boys? Some cosmic mistake had been made.

What did I know about diapering, much less potty-training a boy? What did I know about superheroes? Where did boys learn that vroooing noise, anyway? Not easily tired, I found my sons' energy level daunting, their explorations scary, and their fascination with vehicles unexplainable. A train in a store window could immobilize us for an hour. Rearranging Brio displays in toy shops was an activity good for a lost morning. Happening upon a construction site and the accompanying machinery was an entire afternoon adventure. Creating trenches of mud and water, crisping bugs under magnifying glasses, collecting rodents in cages, all became part of my everyday existence. Their skillful drawings showed action figures in bloody confrontations, or buildings in perfect perspective. Trips to Disneyland became occasions for whiplash and nausea. The fun of dropping, twisting, and turning eluded me. I reluctantly embraced every adventure, just to prove I was up to raising boys.

My mother, the authority on anything motherly, conceded after a week with my sons, "Boys are different." You're darned right. They're not feminine. They didn't nurture dolls. They categorized plastic dinosaurs. They didn't beg to go to the ballet. They put up with obligatory *Nutcracker* performances. No piano woke me on Sunday mornings, but a saxophone and, of all things, drums. Because I didn't know how else to mother boys, I treated them as any liberated woman of the era would, just as I would like to have been treated, and as I hoped their future wives would treat them—like people. I figured if I went over the line of appropriateness, they would tell me. They were tolerant when I imparted all my feminine insights. Still, they grew to be different, to be male.

Sixteen years later I live in the alien territory of testosterone. One of the last moms to be outgrown by my sons, I am lucky to have been so long spared dwarfism. But today, miniature is me. My life is endless muddy laundry, lost objects ("Mom, what did you do with my. . . ?"), and grocery excursions that cause people to ask what army I am buying for. I live in terror of heavy-footed, soon-to-be licensed teenage drivers, and football injuries. Recently, watching a downed player, I confided in another mother: "My son would kill me. It would jeopardize our entire relationship for his whole life, but if he didn't get right up, I'd be out there on the field in a second." She agreed.

Dinner is a time to inhale food. Conversations are infrequent and then usually about sports. "Mom, the most exciting thing is when you make a shot, and you're hit, and you're on the ground, in pain, and you hear the cheering. That's what lacrosse is about," my son said.

"How about if you make the shot, and you hear the cheering, without the ground and pain part?" I asked.

"Not the same," he explained, sighing. Their fighting spirit is in a physical world, of muscle and sweat. The determination, the bravery thrill me. But world crises, troops being dispatched, violence, all the downside of the masculine world, hold a newly defined panic. I have worked too hard to give them away.

"A son's a son till he takes a wife, but a daughter's a daughter the rest of her life." Not once has my mother said that to me since I became the mother of sons, but I grew up believing it. Now, in my own home, I feel hopelessly outnumbered. "I'm home" sounds the same whether it's my boys or their father. Hugs have ceased. Doors are closed. They have entered the territory of manhood. I am not invited.

Still, when we are alone, they describe their world, perhaps as I described mine to them as they were growing up. In some ways it's not so different. When I see the flush of a crush, I feel proud. "Till he takes a wife" doesn't seem like the death knell of our friendship.

Several years ago, when they were still small, when they didn't walk ahead or behind, embarrassed to be with me, we three went to hear Jane Goodall speak on her chimpanzee studies. I sat with my boys, who seemed to be lent to me from a dimension as far away from mine as her jungle laboratory. "In the primate world," she said, "the only relationship that lasts throughout life. . ."—I waited, ready for the inevitable bad news—". . . is the mother-son bond," she finished.

That was the last thing in the world I expected.

SAFETY NET

MY DAD AND I CAN SET our watches by each other. Every Tuesday and Thursday after I drive my son's carpool, I head back to the main street in our town. Rain or shine, between 8:10 and 8:15 a.m., I know I'll spot him carrying a white plastic grocery bag and wearing his oversized orange parka. Most days, he is plugged into his Walkman; my dad is teaching himself Japanese by listening to tapes on his daily five-mile morning walks. He knows we'll run into each other, and he brings me a bag filled with articles and tidbits that he thinks would interest me. I get this plastic "life support" bag at least once a week. When I get home, I open up the bag. Each time its contents differ, but the message is the same—take care of yourself. This week there's a coupon for 50 percent off on film development; articles on breast cancer and the benefits of self-examination, and skin care and vitamins. Once in a while, he finds and cuts out an article about one of my old high school classmates—they're getting married, have received a promotion, are moving out of town or back into town. Although there are times I have felt too busy to go through all the pieces of paper and articles, I realize that this isn't about sharing pieces of paper, it's about sharing pieces of our lives.

I count on my dad being there, wearing his big orange parka and walking with the gait of a teenager. No one would ever believe that he'll celebrate his 80th birthday this fall.

I pull up beside him and he deftly hops in. I count on him being there, and he always is. Together we go to Peet's or Starbuck's to have a cup of coffee and a scone, but more importantly, to connect. Yesterday, we sat at Starbuck's talking about what each of us had planned for the day. "I'm going to a lecture on the UC Berkeley campus, then over to the City," he told me. "They're having the monthly brown bag opera at the Galleria, you know." I had never realized the full life my dad led while I sat at work staring at my computer screen each day. I'm not sure what I thought he did, but I know I didn't think he did so much. I asked him if we could meet again the next day for another cup o' joe. His reply, "I'd love to, but I'm taking a sushi-making class. Can we have lunch instead?"

Although our morning ritual began when I stopped working full-time a little over a year ago, my ability to count on him has been there since I took my first breath.

As a young child, I would sit by the window, staring at the street, until he pulled up in his cherished 1949 Studebaker. When I was growing up, he would spend a few hours each weekend just tinkering around that car. He adorned it with every gizmo invented. I'm sure it was the only car around that had a rear-view mirror that reflected a width of 50 yards. "Better to be safe than sorry," he'd tell me. I was the only one of my friends who, at the age of 13, could change a tire.

His wisdom seemed as unending as his patience. Whenever I brought home school forms that required my parents to list their vocation, I always filled in the line entitled "Father's Occupation" myself. I loved telling my friends what he did. "My dad's a chemist," I would say, bursting with pride.

"You saved the *Chronicle*'s pink section for me, didn't you?" is his usual Tuesday morning question.

"Dad, you know I always do," I say, handing over my own sack of trivia I've gathered for him. Each week my bag for him contains the pink section (of course), some schoolwork from my son (his only grand-child), and usually a clipping of an event I think he may want to attend.

This man, who makes his own jam, takes sea-kayaking lessons, holds the anchor ropes for my son while he rock-climbs, has more volunteer hours at my son's school than I do, yet manages to serve on the board of his mother's nursing home, ushers at any event he can at Zellerbach, and never misses a production of the San Francisco Opera, still makes me feels as if he has all the time in the world for me.

When I was 14, I joined the Girl Sea Scouts, better known as the "Mariners." It was the night before the annual Mariners' Regatta and, with a barely legible photocopy of instructions, I sat on my bed struggling to learn to tie the several types of knots our troop would be tested on the next day. I fell apart on my bed and cried, knowing I'd never memorize all of them by morning. That's when I heard a gentle knocking on my bedroom door.

"Linda, what's the matter?" he asked softly.

"I'll never remember all of this, I can't even tie one single knot," I sobbed.

"Let's just take it one step at a time," he said calmly. "Tell me what you need to know."

He stayed up with me until 2 a.m. that night, teaching me, testing me, until I could tie all of the knots with my eyes shut.

We went on countless walks together as I emerged from childhood to adolescence. It was on these walks that he talked to me about life and choices and consequences. All of the things I have had the courage and the strength to do resulted from the belief he gave me in myself. He was my biggest supporter as I was learning to fly a small plane. He and my mother were on the next available flight from their vacation in Hawaii when my then-husband walked out on me and my young son.

As I find myself in my forties, his care and concern about me have not dissipated. If I need to make a trip, he still asks that I call when I arrive.

Although there have been countless occasions that have made me realize how special a man he is and how very lucky I am, I have never felt more proud of my dad than during the past two months when his 98-year-old mother became ill. He sat by her bedside every day, spoon-feeding her with meals he prepared himself, in an effort to keep her comfortable during her last days. He cared for her until she passed away, never showing signs of exasperation or impatience, even when the call for such human emotion was overdue. His mother taught him the power of kindness and strength, and it was only natural for him to be there for her when she needed him most; he has spent his life passing that wisdom on to me, his only child.

He has always been, and continues to be, there for me. I live my life knowing this, taking strength from it and believing in myself because he so deeply believes in me. He is my anchor, my safety net, and perhaps because I know he stands ready to catch me, I have never been afraid to fall.

Appeared April 22, 2001 in the *San Francisco Chronicle* Living Section, and November 28, 1996 in the *El Cerrito Journal.*

THE SIGHT OF STEAK

Shahnaz Chinoy Taplin

(Note: Bakri Eid *or* Eid-al-adha *is the "festival of sacrifice." It commemorates Abraham's devotion to God and his willingness to sacrifice his son, Ishmael, to God. As Ishmael is being killed, God miraculously substitutes a sheep. Today, Muslims all over the world celebrate this festival by sacrificing a sheep, cow, or camel, and distributing two-thirds of the meat to the poor.)*

DAWN BREAKS. EXCITEMENT MOUNTS as grandparents, uncles, aunts, and grandchildren sense the electricity of *Eid* with their first sip of morning tea. A soft breeze blows through our bedroom window. It looks over the pasture, where a dozen goats chew on their last blades of succulent grass.

A few days before *Eid*, a goat is bought for each member of the family and left to graze in my paternal grandparents' backyard. Posted at the bay window, I stare vacantly for hours at a stretch at the goats— my new playmates. The goats usually stayed close by my window. When they strayed out of sight, I didn't like it. I liked to connect and commune with them. I can still feel their stubby, coarse-haired coats and doe-like eyes as I petted and played with them on scorching, sweaty summer afternoons and mist-moistened mornings.

On *Eid* morning, a quickened tempo permeated an otherwise sleepy family. The male members of the household bathed, dressed, and departed for prayers in an open-air *maidan*. My father, grandfather, uncles, and cousins and the cook, his helper, and the driver would emerge from their baths—cleansed dark princes attired in stiffly-starched, blinding-white cotton pajamas.

While the men were at *Eid* prayers, the family home would become the women's domain. The three daughters-in-law, each a traffic-stopping beauty, bathed and dressed in a discreet cotton sari. Each one celebrated the joy of *Eid*, one on one, with Allah in her heart. This she was entitled to, even though this family caged women, denied them celebrations and smiles. Engulfed in a somber space, daughters-in-law were expected to respond demurely to questions with downcast eyes. The austere tone was set by the chiffon-clad, iron-willed mother-in-law, my grandmother, who presided over the family like a chilling, still-life portrait, poised in her chair with a diamond stud in her nose.

The men soon returned. *Eid mubarak* greetings were exchanged. The grandchildren performed the obligatory ritual and responded to the command performance to kiss our grandmother's hand. It was but a formality, devoid of love and feeling. The ritual feast followed. Aromatic *dal* (lentils) with steaming vapors were spooned onto our plates and served with wheat *chappattis* just hot off the griddle. I can still see, smell, and savor the memory of richly spiced *Eid ki dal*.

I lingered for hours on a spacious verandah which overlooked a well-sculpted garden with rows of luscious red canna, and imbibed tea in tune with the morning rhythms of my grandparents. On these mornings, I saw sumptuous breakfasts being prepared for the *fakir* (beggar) of the day by my father's spinster sister, who was obsessed with being a devout Muslim.

Did my paternal family believe that these activities would secure a place for them in Allah's heaven? Did they really believe that their visible discrimination against servants, favoritism towards beggars, and subjugation of daughters-in-law would be invisible and canceled by their "good deeds of charity"?

The *Eid* feast ends with a core, gut-wrenching ritual. The dozen goats move from the pasture to the front garden and line up, one for each member of the family. Being the youngest, I was the last family member to fulfill the ceremonial rites with my goat. According to the *halal* tradition, the goat was given water, pointed eastward to Mecca, shown his face in a hand-held mirror, and readied for a quick death to the prayer: "In the name of Allah, the Beneficent, the Merciful. . ."

The last rite of death for me was to pet the goat being sacrificed in my name, only seconds before the butcher's slaughtering knife descended on the doe-eyed creature. Dissolving into tears, I trudged up the back stairs engulfed by the heat fumes emanating from the charcoal-burning stoves in the kitchen. Mournfully, I wondered about my betrayal. How could I have fed, petted, and played with the goats for endless hours and then finally killed my *bakra*?

The family believed that I would outgrow the pain of *Eid*; rather, the brutality of the annual slaughter was stamped into my psyche. I can still hear my mother say: "Two-thirds goes to charity—it feeds the poor; a third is for the family—we keep only what we need." And so while my Muslim tradition cherishes meat as central to religion, celebration, and charity, to this day my stomach still curdles at the sight of a steak.

BELGRADE, REVISITED

Rina Alcalay

IN THE EARLY MONTHS OF 1999 Belgrade, the capital of what used to be Yugoslavia, was bombed during the conflict in the Balkan peninsula. In the United States we watched scenes of the bombing on television, and I was particularly glued to the screen. The expression on Belgrade civilians' faces, especially the numb disbelief of older folks, revealed their shock and lack of understanding about why this was happening again in their lifetime. Their faces haunted me and reminded me of my parents' fate as Jewish refugees during that other tragic, not-so-distant period in Yugoslavian history. The flames and horror of the fleeing refugees just a couple of years ago were all too familiar to the generation who lived through the Nazi bombing of Belgrade in 1941.

Wedding bells in Belgrade. The year was 1940. My father and mother united their lives while winds of war blew throughout Europe. They chose an informal wedding style. No elaborate long white dress for my mother who decided instead to wear a tailored cream suit. Only family members were invited to the celebration. After the wedding they settled in the top floor of a downtown building owned jointly by my father and grandfather. A study, dressed in Persian rugs and wood-paneled walls, was furnished as an office for my father, a judge.

Less than a year later, on April 6, 1941, this illusion of normality disintegrated completely. My parents woke up to the sound of German planes dropping bombs over their city. In haste, they packed a suitcase, got my grandparents, and found a taxi driver who, for a large sum of money, drove them amidst the chaos in desperate flight from the burning city.

A harrowing journey followed, from Belgrade to Split in Dalmatia. They decided to go to Dalmatia with the hope that there they would catch a boat that would take them somewhere, away from the Nazis. As they drove on the deserted roads, bombs exploded all around their vehicle. Somehow, miraculously, no bomb hit their taxi. In this journey my parents left behind the peaceful, orderly world that they and their families before them had known for centuries, and initiated the most horrendous period in their lives, and one of the darkest, if not the darkest, periods in the history of the Jewish people, World War II.

In Split they found there was no way out; there were no more ships leaving to go anywhere; the borders were closed. They were trapped. Thus, instead of escaping, my parents became prisoners of the Italian Fascists who interned them in Korcula, an island off the coast of Dalmatia. Two years later, Germany invaded Italian territory and my parents had to find a way to leave Korcula before the Nazis arrived. They escaped during the night, in a small boat, through a German submarine–infested Adriatic Sea, to German-occupied Italy.

My mother developed a strange fever, it came every afternoon— no medical reason for it. One unwanted pregnancy after another had to be ended using risky procedures. They could not afford a baby when forced to hide in the attic of some Northern Italian peasant's house or in haystacks. German soldiers turned every hiding place upside down when they poked the hay with their bayonets.

In World War II my parents lost everything: extended family, friends, professions, properties, identity, the right to a normal life, the right to be human. The war years brought them countless horrors, prison, escape, hunger, terror. Trying to survive, to eat, to hide, to move to the next town, to trust people who for money would assist them to reach the next hiding place, to not lose the will to go on. Four full years, every day of each one of those years spent thinking it was their last.

The year of 1944 found my parents hiding in Rome, living through the generosity of an Italian concierge who disobeyed the strict orders to turn in all *Juden* (Jew) identity papers to the occupying Germans, and who shared the scarce food from her rationing card with them. Finally, the day when the allies liberated Rome arrived—the happiest day in my parents' life. And then, among the victorious allied forces, a most glorious vision: a battalion carrying a flag with the Star of David marching with the British contingent. A Jewish battalion. Their eyes could not believe it. Their hearts swelled with infinite relief and joy. All the tears they had not shed during those years came pouring out. They threw themselves on the Jewish soldiers with an embrace that was unlike any other. Recalling that moment would fill my parents' eyes with tears for the rest of their lives.

Two years later they were living in Milan. My father had a job. Their apartment had become a haven for those few ghostly survivors who, underfed, disoriented, and prematurely aged by the past years, came to rest for a few days. This period brought them the realization of the enormity of their losses. Countless family members—grandparents, cousins, uncles, and aunts with whom so much life had been shared, dear friends—had all been murdered in the camps or in other horrible ways during the past years. There was no going back; their large families who had lived and thrived in the same region for almost five centuries had been extinguished. What was there to live for anymore?

In the building in Milan where my parents lived, the elevator was operated by a cheerful, talkative Italian. My father engaged in daily conversations with him on his way to work, and later on returning from work. He appeared to be a very happy man, in spite of his poverty and lack of education. He told my father about the great joy and pride he derived from being the father of a large number of children. "Children are the greatest treasure," he often told my father. My father wondered how this man could be so happy when he had so many children to feed and such meager resources. My father was inspired.

One day he came back to the apartment and told my mother, "If this poor man feels so rich and happy because of his many children, why do we not have even one? We must have a child, we must reaffirm life, start life over again from under the ashes of our lives." And that is how I came into this world. Shortly after my birth, my parents left Europe for good, and embarked on a journey that would lead them to settle down in South America.

The repeat of war in the region of the former Yugoslavia, now divided into several independent states, makes me wonder about the shortness of human memory and the capacity we humans have to hate, disrupt, uproot, and destroy lives. I ask myself, how can we keep doing such harm to each other? And yet, even after the Holocaust, my parents were given another chance to reaffirm life. The example of their existence also showed me the capacity and courage of human beings to rise from the ashes, and to regenerate. Even though their previous world was destroyed, my parents picked up the pieces of their shattered existences and created, in a new land, meaningful and productive lives for themselves and their children.

Appeared July 1999 in *The Jewish Bulletin of Northern California.*

TRANSITIONS

BRIDES

Ellen Hauptli

#1: ERIC AND I CAME BACK TO BERKELEY for our nuptial summer after living in San Diego and before moving to New York City. I was a bride in Berkeley. We held the wedding at the home of the friends for whom we were housesitting. All of our furniture, pots, and most clothes were in storage until the actual move to New York. But the one thing I couldn't part with was my sewing machine. Even though we were only in Berkeley for the summer, I was, after all, growing my business by making and selling elegant pleated clothing.

So when it came time to have our own wedding, I was prepared: borrowed house, friends to take photos, family to bring food, a stack of fabric, and a short rack of pleated clothes. After hand-printing our invitations (literally—our palms were purple for days!) and hiring the marrier, I set to work sewing Eric's wedding shirt. Then he went out and bought a pair of slacks and a professional haircut to go with the shirt. I chose my wedding dress straight from my rack. It was a pleated cream strapless dress with green buttons down the front, and a wispy silk vest, hand-painted by an artist friend.

Friends and relations convened as requested on our wedding day, each one bringing their specialty: camera, flowers, food, champagne. It seemed one of my friends also brought her jealousy. She herself was unhappy and couldn't cope in such close proximity to joy. First, she upset an entire shelf of dishes. Later, after our vows were smoothly and

successfully exchanged, she slipped, spilling a glass of champagne on
a friend who was wearing one of my pleated dresses. But it didn't
matter. The pleats aren't bothered by cool liquids.

Later still and in front of everyone, this friend spoke long and
loudly about how happy Eric and I looked. Then she slipped again and
dumped steaming hot coffee on the front of my dress. Pleats don't hold
up under heat, they become deformed. But it didn't matter, I just went
to my rack and donned another pleated gown, the one I called an
"instant dress." It was a good invention for the dampening of dresses
(but not spirits) at weddings.

#2: SHE FLEW ALL THE WAY FROM SEATTLE with her third husband-to-be
just to consult with me about her wedding dress and the bridesmaid
dresses of her daughter (from her first marriage) and her stepdaughters-
to-be. It seemed like an extravagant trip to me, but they balanced it by
coming to Berkeley from the airport via public transportation. This
bride, Kate, had passed through Berkeley to do some clothes shopping
in my studio a few years ago with her second husband. She had just
married him and they were moving to Seattle together. Eric remembered
that they were too lovey-dovey and that the groom had red hair. Eric
didn't think the marriage would last. He was right. Kate told me in our
pre-trip phone conversation that it hadn't worked out with Angus, they
had gone their separate ways. But now she had the right guy, Tom.

When Kate and Tom came, we spent time looking at styles and
colors. Of course Kate tried on several outfits, some for herself and
some for the girls. Tom was marginally interested in the clothes but was
polite and helped make some color decisions for the daughters. He was
not at all lovey-dovey and he had salt-and-pepper hair—good signs for
Kate, I thought. After a while, Tom stepped outside to play with my
dog as Kate's and my plans were worked out. She found her wedding
dress in the studio: a long two-piece in cream with white chiffon
frostings on the hem and shoulders. I was on my knees measuring the
hem when Tom leaned in the door and said, "Say, Ellen, I hear Kate
brings all her husbands here."

#3: WHAT A NICE COUPLE! Janet and Jim came to my spring studio sale

looking for wedding clothes. Both of them were born in Texas and "born wearing jeans," Janet said, so shopping for a wedding dress would be quite an adventure. Everyone present, including other shoppers, wanted to help Janet choose something wonderful. When we learned the wedding would take place on a ranch in Austin where as a teenager Jim had worked as a roper, we discouraged Janet from choosing white. Then we found out she had turquoise and pink cowboy boots, and that a mariachi band would play for the celebration. By then, Janet had all kinds of personal dressers fluttering around her, putting together ensemble after ensemble for such a fiesta. While modeling the tenth outfit for Jim, she let slip that the two of them had been living together for 27 years already! We kept dressing her, now in awe. She tried the coral, the blue, the spruce, the purple, and the spruce again. This last was made of uneven layers of deep turquoise chiffon in two different kinds of pleats with a wrap of pieced and pleated bright prints. Everyone approved and this was the wedding dress she settled on. She could even wear the boots with it.

Janet was very happy with her choice, though she worried about how to break it to her mother who had been sending her clippings from *Bride* magazine. As the hubbub died a little and Janet returned to her jeans, she and Jim were standing together about to pay when someone asked the inevitable question: "Why are you getting married after 27 years?" Janet threw her hands to her cheeks and exclaimed, "I don't know! I just proposed to him on Christmas Day, and he said yes!"

ANGEL RESURRECTED

Linda Goldfarb

SHE STARED AT ME from the cardboard box; she didn't look as threatening as she had ten years earlier. I gently lifted her from the crumpled tissue and held her up. She wasn't very big, perhaps 10 or 12 inches high. Her dark-green velvet gown, tattered and faded with age, disguised the stand designed to keep her erect on top of the tree.

"We've come a long way," I thought to myself as I dusted her off.

It began during our first Christmas as a "blended" family. We were on our way to buy our first tree together. My son and I had always bought a small tree; my new husband and his children had always bought a large tree.

My husband, myself, my five-year-old son Chris, and my husband's children—eight-year-old Emilie and 12-year-old Seth— piled into the car. There was tension in the air as we all tried to figure out how we fit together.

We entered the tree lot and immediately our group divided. My son and I veered toward the four- to five-foot trees that we had traditionally purchased. My husband and his children headed to the back of the lot where the large trees were displayed.

"Mom, look, I found a great one," Chris called to me. I went over to him, all the while searching for my husband and his children who were nowhere to be seen.

"That's a great tree, but let's see if we can find everyone else to make sure they like it too." Chris scampered off to find them while the salesperson put a "hold" tag on the tree. By the time I found the rest of our group, Chris's eyes were red and he was barely holding back tears. I looked up at my husband, "What's wrong?" I asked.

"Chris told us he found a tree, but Seth and Emilie found a tree they like, too," said Steve, my tactful husband of five months. I looked over—and up—and saw Emilie and Seth standing next to an enormous tree.

"Our angel will look so pretty on top of this tree. I can't wait to put all our decorations on it," said Emilie. My husband looked at me imploringly. "We've always gotten the kids a big tree. It's sort of tradition," he said, looking quite uncomfortable.

I felt my son pulling on my coat. "Mom, what about the tree I found?"

And so it began. I explained to Chris that Steve and his kids had been getting big trees for many years and that the living room would look beautiful with the large tree. He nodded his head, but tears again filled his eyes.

The big tree was purchased and delivered. Chris and I brought out our box of ornaments, and my husband and his children brought out their boxes of decorations.

"Where's our angel?" Emilie asked her father. "I can't find her anywhere."

"It should be in one of these boxes," he replied as he tried to untangle several strands of lights.

"We don't have an angel, but we have a gold star we used to use," I offered.

"No, we *always* put our angel on top," she declared. "We can't put just anything on top—we *have* to find our angel," she insisted. I bristled each time she said the word "angel." "Maybe mom has it."

"No, your mother took half the ornaments, but she left the angel. Believe me, I remember," Steve said in a disgusted tone. Apparently the angel held more significance than I realized. I found myself resenting the doll.

"Why don't we buy a new angel?" I suggested. Emilie glared at me.

The tree sat topless for a week while the house was searched.

Finally, my husband convinced Emilie that perhaps we should buy a new angel for the tree. She reluctantly agreed to go shopping with me and Chris in search of a replacement but insisted that we find one exactly like their old one. She rejected each one Chris or I found.

"Here's a pretty one," I said and showed them a doll-like figure in a white lace gown with a delicate porcelain face holding a tiny white light in her hand. "I like her," Chris said. "Okay, fine," Emilie snapped.

The new angel was purchased and placed on top of the tree. "It's just not the same," Emilie complained. "Where's *our* angel?"

We knew she wasn't just talking about the angel. She did want to find their angel, but more than that, she wanted her old family back. Each loss of tradition was another painful reminder. Every attempt on my part to bring a piece of our life into theirs was met with resistance. "That's not how *we* do it," I was constantly reminded by his children.

The following Christmas, as I was getting out the decorations, I spotted a dusty old box in the back of the closet. I pulled it out and lifted the lid. There she was—their Christmas angel. I replaced the lid and put the box back deep in the closet. That night I confessed to my husband that I had found the angel. "Let it stay in the box, don't say anything, I'm sure she's forgotten about it" was his advice. But when it came time to trim the tree, she again brought up the angel. Neither her father nor I said a word, and the new angel was placed on top of the tree.

It was a difficult process to fit into their family and into their home. For the first three years, my son always called the house "Steve's house." "Are we going to Steve's house?" he would ask. "No, honey, we're going home, it's our home, too." What I didn't want to admit was that I felt the same way. Little by little, more of our knickknacks were brought out, and as time passed, they were met with less resistance. We were both looking for a way to feel we were home.

Each holiday season, the tree took on more of a blended look. During the early years, we had to search for a familiar ornament; but as the holidays came and went, we bought more decorations together and the tree became less "yours" or "mine" and more "ours." We had agreed on a compromise of alternating years of the big tree and the not-so-big tree, and as time passed, I noticed that the size of the tree didn't seem to matter anymore. The kids would search the rows together to find just the right tree. But, as the new angel was placed on top of the tree each year, there was an uneasiness between my husband and myself.

As the kids grew older, the tension dissipated. "I was really awful to live with those first few years, wasn't I?" Emilie said to me last year.

"It wasn't easy for any of us," I admitted.

"But do you remember the fuss I made over that silly Christmas angel? How could you stand me?"

"I wasn't much better, and I was an adult," I admitted to her.

When I began getting out the decorations for Christmas last year, I again came across the dusty cardboard box in the back of the closet. I hesitated for a moment, then pulled it out.

"Emilie, Chris, Seth," I called, "look what I found in the back of the closet."

They came running into the room. Emilie's eyes lit up as she saw me open the box.

"The angel, you found her!" She was elated, then paused. "But what will we do with our new angel? We can't just put her away."

"We can put a hook on her dress and hang her on a branch near the top of the tree. She'll look fine there."

"Or," Emilie suggested, "we can alternate years for each angel to be on top, just like we did with the size of the tree."

"That's a great idea," Chris chimed in.

We've come such a long way, I thought to myself.

"Come on," I said, "let's put the original angel on top this year. She's been hibernating a long time."

As I reached the top of the ladder, Emilie handed her to me and I gently placed the tattered angel on top of the tree.

Finally, I knew we were home.

Appeared December 24, 2000 in the First Person section of the *San Francisco Chronicle*.

NECESSITY IS THE REINVENTION
OF MOTHER

Elizabeth Fishel

WHEN THE PHONE RINGS AT NOON, I still wonder if it's one of my teenage sons calling from school (collect, of course), needing forgotten homework or a pair of basketball shoes for a big game. I'm still packing lunches, tracking socks, quizzing vocabulary words from acme to zenith. Although my sons and I have long since turned the corner from sagging diapers to sagging jeans, trikes to driving tests, and 2 a.m. feedings to 2 a.m. returns home, I've already started the long slide away from being the center of their lives. All too soon, they'll no longer be the center of mine.

No more Saturday morning back-to-back soccer games. No more parent conferences, school bake sales, and teacher gifts for the holidays. No more kids jumping on our just-made bed or dropping laundry on the bathroom floor. Although I've belly-ached about every one of these things, as my sons will be the first to tell you, now that they're threatening to end, each soccer goal and laundry pile, each school meeting and progress report suddenly seems precious. I've seen the future, and if it doesn't include my sons, who will I be?

With the children of midlife baby boomers starting to leave home in droves (about four million turned 18 in 2001, up from 3.3 million in 1993), many of us are or soon will be facing this life passage, this jolt to psyche and self-definition. Many of us adult daughters remember our own mothers facing our inevitable dance away from home and the resulting Empty Nest with anguish, clinginess, or deep regrets.

"Remember you've been your mother's whole life," my father whispered to me during my first visit home from college, pleading with me to be patient, while I vainly tried to wriggle out from my mother's grasp. But unlike our own mothers, my friends and I, lucky inheritors of feminism's options, have been multitasking for years. We've prided ourselves on all the roles we've juggled besides motherhood—caring wives, dutiful daughters, competent professionals, devoted friends, community activists, and seekers of self-awareness. But now we, too, find we need to reinvent ourselves just as surely as our mothers did.

Although I'm not quite there yet, I watch as my older friends negotiate this razor's edge. Each flounders and tries to cope in her own distinctive way. Marion's 18-year-old daughter moved out three months ago, and Marion, a gifted teacher, gives her a daily wake-up call to make sure she's up for her job. Christine won't admit that her children's growing up means she's getting older, too, and spends hours at the gym trying to maintain the taut body she had half a lifetime ago. Karen, a successful therapist and work-life expert, sinks into a blue funk, as her children's leaving home leaves her adrift and stirs up troubling memories of her own uneasy childhood separations.

I watch my friends as they try to buffer themselves against the inevitabilities of the next stage with strategies that don't quite work. But then slowly I begin to see them struggling to find the gain in loss, the path out of the thicket from one identity to the next. Marion lets go of the daily habit of mothering and finds the time to start Italian classes and plan a sabbatical year with her husband in a small Tuscan town. Once cloistered in the gym, Christine finds a new coterie of women fitness friends of all ages and shapes, and expands her horizons biking and hiking with them in the hills. Karen resumes her practice of meditation, long abandoned when her children were small and needy, and connects with a spiritual center for weekend retreats. Each emerges from the crucible of separation newly redefined, more focused, more energetic, more herself.

Still a mother of teenagers, I savor my last remaining years of child-raising—each family dinner, each heart-to-heart, each birthday celebration taking on a special luster but also a poignancy which they never had when my boys' growing up seemed to stretch out endlessly into the future. Watching my friends up-end their lives and emerge anew, I both fear and anticipate the stage beyond motherhood and try to ready the ground for my next incarnation. I expand my writing groups, enroll in a poetry class, plan a literary event to raise money to fight breast cancer, the disease that recently took my mother's life. I start jumping rope on the back deck to make a dent in my thickening waist. I reconnect with several old friends and make dinners for others who are going through difficult times. When I wake in the middle of the night and find that my husband is up, too, I ask him gently what's on his mind and see if we can go through this together, readying ourselves for the gift of reinvention, the energy of the second chance.

A RITE OF PASSAGE

Lori Rosenthal

THE SHOPPING SPREE BEGAN like any other shopping spree. We walked into the store, selected a shopping cart, and started careening through the aisles. Grandma took the nine-year-old off in pursuit of bellbottom jeans. I searched for lightweight shorts with deep pockets. In short time, our carts were full and we both found ourselves in the dressing room.

The routine was familiar. Take off whatever you were wearing when you entered the store. Put on whatever it was that caught your eye. The nine-year-old was trying on pair after pair of blue jeans rimmed with colorful tapestry-like materials. I was trying on shorts, shorts, and more shorts. Grandma was taking things off and putting them back on hangers.

With this scene as the backdrop, a conversation began.

Nine-year-old: "Mom, the fifth-grade girls say I need a bra."

Me: "Sweetie, you don't need a bra."

Nine-year-old: "Well, they say I do."

Me: "Do you think you do?"

Nine-year-old: "I don't know but they say so."

Throughout this conversation, we kept our rhythm of trying on items and placing them in the keep or discard piles. Grandma kept up the steady activity of rehanging the garments as needed. We dressed and undressed in silence. The wheels in my head were cranking away.

I remembered back to my seventh-grade year, when three

adolescent girls became fast friends simply for the reason that we were all still flat-chested when the rest of our classmates were not. I remember to this day the many embarrassing, pleading conversations I had had with my mother on the topic of could I or could I not buy a bra. She finally relented when my chest began to reshape itself. But I was among the last girls in my gym class to wear a bra. It was not a pleasant memory. It had not been a pleasant experience.

I restarted the conversation.

Me: "Do you want to try on a bra today?"

Nine-year-old (emphatically): "*No*."

Me: "Are you sure? We're here and I could easily go get one for you."

Nine-year-old (less emphatically): "No."

Meanwhile, we added a great pair of blue jeans and two pairs of perfect shorts to the keep pile. It was a good shopping trip and we were getting dressed to go home.

She restarted the conversation tentatively.

Nine-year-old: "Mom, maybe I could try on a bra."

Me: "Want to?"

Nine-year-old: "Sort of."

Me (suppressing a smile): "Okay."

We got dressed and exited the dressing room holding hands, headed for the lingerie section. We got there and found the rack with small sizes. We immediately saw the perfect choice: a sports bra— kind of a cropped undershirt with an elastic bottom. I took two off the rack and handed them to her. She looked around the store as if she had done something wrong and handed them right back to me. I guess I was going to carry them back to the dressing room.

At the dressing room, I handed the attendant the two bras and got my plastic card with the number 2. My daughter hung back as if she didn't know me, face beet-red and quite visibly uncomfortable. I turned to her and asked, "Want to come in with me?" "Sure," she responded.

It took less than 15 seconds for her to rip off her shirt and slip the bra over her head. It took close to 15 minutes for her to admire it from all angles in the three-way mirror. During that time, I was able to go in and out twice, try on two bathing suits, find her younger sister and get her to try on some shirts. Each time the dressing room door opened, the nine-year-old was mortified that someone might see her. Yet each time the door closed and locked she once again began to preen.

The two bras went in the keep pile along with the other items we were taking home. The bathing suits and shirts went into the reject pile. I handed the bras to her to carry out of the dressing room. She handed them right back to me. I looked at her and smiled. No more words were exchanged. She slipped her hand in mine and we exited the dressing room together. She gave my hand a small squeeze. She was walking a bit taller and her face was radiant. The shopping spree that began like any other ended as a day etched in both our memories.

LETTING GO

Diana Divecha

AGAINST THE DISTURBING BACKDROP of unresolved kidnappings, reports on teen predators, and my summer reading of a bestseller about a teenager's horrifying rape, death, and afterlife, I tried to prepare my 14-year-old daughter for high school. In September, Zai would be leaving the safety of my vigilant supervision to take the BART for high school in another city an hour from home. Over the summer she had practiced small steps toward independence: forays downtown with friends, a supervised BART ride. But a regular daily commute, solo, from Berkeley to South San Francisco was still a qualitative leap.

The night before the first day of school, I helped her make an ID and an in-case-of-emergency-card for her wallet and together we figured out her schedule. She arranged travel times with friends, and I ruled that her cell phone must be charged and carried at all times. As she packed up her book bag, I asked her how she felt about the first day of school. She said she had a "wait-and-see attitude," neither excited nor scared. I was awed by her equanimity. It's not the first time I was struck by her serenity, her reasonableness—she was the child who was born quiet, eyes wide open, as if fully cognizant. And she has rarely wavered since, although surely some naiveté helps, I thought to myself. As for me? I was fencing in my anxiety, desperate not to infect her with it while also arming her with safety strategies.

Later that night, I cracked. In the privacy of my own room, I cried and cried, though it was the confused tears of not knowing why I was crying. Free-floating despair is the worst kind. I thought it was about my own life: my lack of time, no one appreciates me, my-life-is-worthless, a downward spiral. Somewhere in my review of life's deficits, I accidentally hit on how scared I was for my daughter, and then I really started wailing. "Bingo!" my rational mind whispered. The full force of my fear found me.

The first morning she left for school, I instructed Zai to call when she arrived. She didn't. I tried her cell phone in vain for 45 minutes, then I called my husband to help me decide whether to let my fear or my rational mind dominate. He said, "She might feel undermined if you call the school," so I finally accepted that it was statistically improbable that something terrible would happen on the first day. I made it through the day subdued, then ecstatic (but proffering cool) on her return. She had managed the trip just fine, and in the noise and excitement of talking with new travel companions she had simply not heard her phone ring. I gave up the confirmation-call requirement.

Subsequent days unfolded, and each time she emerged from the station at four o'clock, I exhaled. Soon the image of my umbilical cord stretching down into the BART tube and across the bay faded. Each evening she shared stories of her new experiences: lunchtime gatherings, advisory, new teachers, clubs. But buried in the day's story was a zinger. I'm sure she was simply asking for my help to assess risk, a small part of an otherwise cheerful report, but every comment spiked my adrenaline: "Today my friends and I took the wrong train home but we changed in West Oakland" (a high crime area). "Oh, my adviser said not to carry a wallet because there have been some muggings near the school." "We've been told what streets to avoid, exactly where to cross to the BART station from school, I went off-campus for lunch today, I'm coming home late today, we can't walk around the outside of campus except in a group, the BART broke down right before going under the bay. . ."

"Ommmmmmmmm," I breathed to myself.

As the school year goes on, I take one day at a time, remaining vigilant where I have control, seeing my daughter off every morning and making sure my last words to her are of love and joy, and gradually letting go and trusting her in the spaces in between. But ask me how I am, and it is my topic of conversation—I am dissipating my anxiety wherever I can, describing ruefully that I am living through my daughter's commute to the city. In spite of myself, I listen to other people's reactions to help me gauge my sanity and guilt. After the bank teller made the mistake of asking me how I was and hearing my tale, she confided back to me, "You know, I drive my 12-year-old to her friend's house and they walk the block to school together—do you think that's all right?" An older friend with successful, grown children said to me that some days she thought it an accomplishment simply to get her children to adulthood alive and reasonably healthy. A mother at my younger daughter's school asked me to drive her sixth-grade son's bike home—she let him bike to school with a friend via a prescribed route, but wouldn't let him bike home alone. A couple I met at a party vigorously debated with each other in front of me whether to let their son bike to BART or whether they should drive him there.

I am so cheered and buoyed to be in good company. All around me are subversive mothers determined to foster their children's independence in spite of their own fears and the constant drumbeat of real threats reported daily in the news. We're all banking on the odds being in our favor and the importance of our children's gradual steps to self-reliance. We are pressing on regardless.

One of the great Buddhist teachers, Thich Nhat Hanh, describes the suffering and sadness we experience because of the constantly changing nature of life. He writes in *No Fear, No Death*: "Thanks to impermanence, everything is possible. Life itself is possible. If a grain of corn is not impermanent, it can never be transformed into a stalk of corn. If your daughter is not impermanent, she cannot grow up to become a woman. Then your grandchildren would never manifest. So instead of complaining about impermanence, we should say, 'Warm welcome and long live impermanence.' We should be happy. When we can see the miracle of impermanence, our sadness and suffering will pass."

And what is happening in the spaces between my vigilance? My daughter's joy is leaking out like bubbles from a champagne glass. "Today there were eight of us riding home together. We all exchanged phone numbers and did text messaging all the way home." "I met a new person I really like." "I met a nice girl in my art class today." "The juniors and seniors who led our orientation are friendly to me in the halls." "An older Spanish student said to let her know if I needed protection on the BART" (smiling and catching my eye). "I went off-campus for lunch today with three other people." "I really like my art class." "My adviser is hilarious." "I love this school." "I never thought I would like a school better than my old one." "People are so nice here."

My daughter's growth curve matches my letting-go curve.

WHERE SOCKS COME FROM

Terri Hinte

MY FIRST PAID JOB, at 12, was as a church organist, and subsequent jobs in and around film, theater, and music would seem to lead in a smooth, inevitable arc toward my present long-term tenure in record business publicity.

But there was one "position" I held, in the summer between high school graduation and college, that doesn't quite fit into this artsy résumé. For those three months, I earned minimum wage as an assembly line worker in a sock factory in Lynchburg, Virginia. I stacked and stickered socks.

As my high school career was blessedly winding to a close and the time arrived to select a summer job, I was disinclined to join my former classmates in the typical temporary slots they'd chosen: perky Republican salesgirls at the Miller & Rhoads department store, wearing their tiny-floral shirtwaist dresses, shellacked bobs, and tangerine lipstick. I leaned toward something more proletarian, where I could stick my waist-length hair insolently into a leather clip and not have to disguise my outré taste in clothes. I didn't want to have to paste a smile on my face and serve anyone, particularly the drawling denizens of Lynchburg, so many of whom had made my life less than pleasant in the two years since I'd been uprooted from my New York home. So it was going to be me and socks in the 100-year-old brick factory, located on a leafy street near the heart of this small Southern city.

I showed up at the factory one warm spring day to apply for work, not having the faintest idea what that work might entail. A tall bespectacled woman from the manager's office escorted me to a small white room with a couple of tables and an assortment of chairs. Half a dozen applicants, men and women, were already seated there, filling out forms. As I scribbled in the requested data, it occurred to me that nothing I'd ever done or hoped to do bore any relevance whatsoever to possible functions I might fill here. Good grades in school? Meaningless. Church organist? Studied French and Latin? Absolutely useless!

What did matter was some mild degree of manual dexterity, and to determine our aptitude a test was administered. I became a little nervous at the prospect: what if I failed to qualify as a sock worker?! Others in the room were nervous, too, even while performing the simple coordination tasks required of us. We had to put small balls and cubes into like-sized and -shaped openings—nothing as difficult as pick-up sticks or Lego construction. More like toddlers' toys.

After the tests and forms were completed, we waited in the white room for further word. The tall woman appeared at the door.

"Miz *Hee*-yunt," she announced, mauling my name. A job was offered to me, and I accepted. She read out the names of two or three other new hirees. The rest didn't make the cut. What kind of work might they look for next?

By the first week of June, summer had arrived in a big, steaming way, and I was spending my days in a factory that was ten degrees hotter than whatever the weatherman was reporting. But it was still somewhat cool when my workday began. Everyone had to punch in by 7 a.m. sharp, when the factory whistle gave a long, bloodcurdling shriek; a minute's tardiness would result in docked pay.

On that first day I arrived, thankfully, with only a minute to spare; I'd walked the eight blocks or so from home not knowing exactly how long the trip would take.

Mr. Blankinship, the ruddy, balding foreman, directed me and three other new workers to our assembly line, where we joined four savvy veterans. He explained the mechanics involved. A "feeder" stood at the head of the line ("the *lahn*"), scooping up socks from boxes, or wherever they came from, and placing them one pair at a time onto the conveyor belt. The feeder's was the most important task, because she paced the workers: she was able to control the speed of the *lahn* from slow enough for you to make some mistakes and still correct them to so fast that you couldn't do a single thing. (Shades of Lucille Ball in the candy factory.)

As the feeder placed a pair of socks on the belt, it passed through a hot-iron wringer contraption that stamped information on one sole—the size, "Made in U.S.A.," and all the other type that disappears the first time the socks are thrown in the washer.

Three women on each side of the belt handled the socks as they glided down the *lahn*. One would stack the socks three pair at a time—that's what she'd do the live-long day. Her counterpart on the opposite side stacked two piles of threes into one pile of six. The next two workers were ankle-stickers, a very tricky business: alternating stacks of six, they'd affix a sticker, usually gold-colored and in the shape of a starburst about an inch in diameter, to the ankle area of *each* top-sock in the stack. And the hardest job of all was reserved for the cuff-stickers: affixing a long, rectangular sticker around and over the cuffs of each pair of socks in the six-stack.

Finally, the "bander" wrapped and taped a white paper band around each stickered stack, and the "boxer" (a college-age boy and the only male on the line) put them in boxes of a half-dozen stacks each and hauled the boxes out to the loading dock.

While we were learning the ropes, the sticker work, especially on important jobs, was reserved for the old-timers like Hazel, who'd been employed at the sock factory for 25 years. Built like a fireplug, Hazel was sassy and vain about her black bouffant hair. She was also fond of red lipstick, which she applied frequently to her thin lips and her Kool cigarette filters.

Most of us stood while working, but Hazel's legs couldn't manage. She sat on a stool, the rolled tops of her stockings exposed. But she was such a pro when it came to stickers, she could've done the work standing on her head.

The stickers themselves came in pads of a hundred or so, and tended to stick together in a gluey mess, particularly in the summer

heat. But Hazel had never met a sticker she couldn't beat into sub-
mission. She'd pick up a new pad and her knowing hands would take
a reading of its physical characteristics: how many times it needed to be
slapped hard against the edge of the belt, how vigorously to riffle the
stickers from one direction to the other and for how long.

Day in and day out, as the socks streamed relentlessly toward her
like cars on a crowded freeway, she'd calmly grab a stack and, with the
grace and delicacy of a raccoon unwrapping a box of food, she'd stick
those stickers where they were supposed to be stuck—in seconds flat.
Hazel made it seem as easy as sighing.

"Child, you just get 'customed to it," she assured us newcomers.

Our assembly line was located on the ground floor of the two-story
building, right next to a big window that looked out on the sidewalk
and street traffic, on the maple trees that occasionally rustled with
summer breezes. Even with the window opened wide, though, very little
air seemed to come our way. The factory held heat like an efficient
oven. Most days, sweat beaded on my face; my scalp dampened and my
hair curled; my sleeveless cotton dresses stuck to my body. That rare
cool breeze provided the briefest respite.

But socks didn't suffer from the weather. They just kept coming
down that line.

Everyone's favorites were the men's athletic socks, usually white
with a few colored stripes at the cuff. With their hefty vertical ribs and
terry soles, they were thick and tractable, easy to manipulate. Not so
men's dress socks, the dark knee-highs men wear so their skin won't
show when they cross their legs and their trousers ride up. These were
lightweight, sheer and slithery, simply impossible to get any kind of
grip on, much less stack. Kay, the unflappable feeder, always had to
slow the line down to a relative crawl for the slippery socks; otherwise
we'd just make a mess.

Sometimes we made a mess anyway—stickers on crooked, even
halfway up the sock! That's when Mr. Blankinship would make an
appearance, his color deepening to a fearsome lobster-red.

"Y'all are gonna have to straighten up," he'd scold with contempt
while sweating like the rest of us, his white shirt sticking to his pot-
belly. "This here's *not* gonna pass muster."

He'd pause, letting the words hang menacingly in the air. When he sensed that they'd penetrated, instilling the desired anxiety and shame, he'd turn his back to us and walk away in that duck-style of his. Sometimes we'd sit awkwardly, looking down at our fidgety hands; then Kay would rev up the feeder again, sending socks our way. But occasionally, once Mr. B. was out of earshot, we'd dissolve in giggles, especially if his rebuke had to do with a difficult slippery-sock job. We might as well have tried to stack and sticker blobs of quicksilver!

One afternoon, just after the Fourth of July weekend, we were on break. Hazel had told us right at the start that we were never to put any food on the belt, which was mottled from years of glue and sweat. "Child," she'd warned, "the *cock*roaches will take your lunch a*way* from you!"

Mindful of her words, I sat next to the window, trying for a breeze, nibbling on a hard, dense brownie from the vending machine. Jean, a girl about my age, was quietly reading, her newspaper spread out on the conveyor belt. The month before, she'd begun working alongside her mother Darcy, one of the line veterans. Every day they drove 35 miles to the factory, all the way from Big Island, the paper mill town. I'd passed through there once with my family, and we had to hold our noses from the stench, even with the car windows shut.

"Listen here," said Jean, her voice rising above the factory's motorized din. "'Rolling Stones guitarist Brian Jones found dead.'"

"He *died*?!" I turned from the window and looked straight at her.

"Says he drowned in a swimming pool. 27 years old."

I absorbed the grim news silently. Jean turned the page of her paper, past other stories of the day—Vietnam casualties, civil rights demonstrations. She didn't read them aloud.

It surprised me that Jean knew or cared enough about the Rolling Stones to share this news with me or anyone; she was usually listening to a country music station. But I had once cared about them a great deal. Five years earlier, at the tender age of 12, I had made their acquaintance—on the radio, in a teen magazine—and was mesmerized by their disheveled randiness and the raw pulsing danger of their music. It was as though a curtain had been torn open, revealing a brand-new world of beckoning darkness and magic and unbridled sexuality. I was in thrall to the view.

My friends and I became fans—short, of course, for "fanatics"—and attended all the Stones' New York shows, when they were still playing dingy little theaters on 14th Street. There a sort of mass hysteria was unleashed. Some kind of contact was sought by the girls in the audience, some communion. A transformation.

I went as far as buying a shirt for Brian's birthday, purchased with my meager church-organ earnings, and sent it off to a fan club address in exotic London. Several weeks later, a handwritten letter of thanks arrived, in a blue-ballpoint backhand, from Brian himself: "I had a lovely birthday. . . the shirt is just my size and colour. . . it's been so wonderful. . . bye bye for now," and so on. I read the letter over and over, as if it contained a vital message for me that eventually I'd be able to decode.

Our teachers noticed our infatuation, and were not pleased. Sister St. Edward made that clear one day as I stood stranded at the blackboard, unable to diagram a subordinate clause.

"Teresa," she hissed, "the Rolling Stones won't pass your exams for you."

No, I thought, but they'll save me from the likes of *you*.

And they did. Real life soon intervened, including real boys and real travails, such as my two-year ordeal in this Southern hell-hole, now drawing to a close. But I'd been fundamentally altered by my exposure to the Rolling Stones. They stood with me at ground zero of my personal cultural revolution, as the shocking realization sank in that my life was veering inexorably off the tidy path charted by parents, teachers, and the Pope.

For a short spell the Stones were gods to me, immortal. Now beautiful blond Brian had come to a dissolute end at the bottom of a swimming pool, and I was still here, about to emerge from my chrysalis and try on this new life he'd shown me a glimmer of.

The summer passed. The socks kept coming. My sticker technique improved, though I could never hold a candle to Hazel. I was amazed at the variety of socks we worked on, and all the things that had to be done to them. When in stores, I'd visit the sock departments and appraise the merchandise: there were the dreaded slippery socks with stickers on the ankles *and* cuffs! This stamp was off-center; that sticker was dead-on. My training was taking hold.

But I knew this wasn't where I belonged. I'd indulged my *nostalgie de la boue*, and by the time September rolled around I was bidding my co-workers adieu and heading for Greenwich Village, for college and extracurricular activities in the mysterious world beyond the curtain, the one the Stones had initiated me into.

As I packed my just-bought socks, I eyed them with a new appreciation. I'd already removed the stickers, but the printing on the sole would remain till the first washing, after which the socks would never be as plush and snug again. No, they'd never be the same.

BRINGING HOME THE BROWN RICE

June Anne Baker

I KNEW THAT NEITHER ONE OF US was totally liberated when we got married. But I also knew that I was more partially-liberated than my husband was. And I knew it wasn't neutral that neither of us cooked. I was at least conscious of what that meant.

His mom had been one of those fine Jewish mothers who actually thrived on domesticity and raising her children. She was a great cook. Meals simply appeared when John was growing up. He didn't know how.

His first wife, a well-organized Virgo, was also a good cook. While she eventually rebelled and became a therapist, she buffered him from the realities of meal preparation during their years together.

When I met him, John wasn't exactly used to carrying his share of the domestic load in the food department. He shared the traditional male's idea that all there was to bringing home the bacon was bringing home money, a notion that overlooks the essential activities of shopping for the bacon, frying it, and washing the pan afterward.

So, one of my self-preservation strategies upon marrying this wonderful but domestically impaired man was to make sure that what we did for food, we did together. Since we lived in a neighborhood blessed with restaurants, most of what we did was leave the house each evening around 6:30 or 7:00 and decide where we were going to go for dinner. We could choose from Chestnut Street or Union Street establishments. I made sure that he picked the restaurant a full 50 percent of the time. Then we would split the bill.

That plan worked really well for dinners, and we ate lunches apart, but there was breakfast. We needed cereal and eggs for breakfast. We needed paper towels and toilet paper and Tide, the other things that grocery stores sell. I made sure that we went grocery shopping together, too. It came down to a once-a-month run to Safeway in the middle of the night. We would leave the house around 10:30 and get to the store when it was least busy, sail through the aisles selecting our staples, and come home.

Of course the Marina Safeway was known as a place to meet singles, and there were fewer singles at that hour, but we were married now and no longer needed shopping to augment our social lives. We'd shop for 45 minutes, and within an hour we'd be unloading our month's supply of dry goods, putting frozen orange juice and waffles into the refrigerator.

We would make occasional midmonth runs for milk and bananas and coffee, but we fell into a pattern where monthly shopping worked fine. There were a few comments from John's sister about "poor John" having to eat out all of the time, but I knew that this approach was actually protecting our marriage. John adjusted easily to restaurants making the food appear, and I didn't resent his lack of participation in meal preparation. I figured this tactic was easier than trying to get John to actually like grocery shopping after four decades of avoiding it.

I would leave it to the next generation of wives to find a more equitable and home-based method of sharing the food work. These younger women might even find husbands who were raised by liberated parents who taught them how to grocery shop and cook. I wasn't exactly smug about our arrangement, but I was self-satisfied enough to ignore the surprised gasps of friends—"You mean you really eat out all of the time?" Well, most of the time. We enjoyed good conversation with no dishes.

Now this was all working very well for the first seven years of our marriage, when I was suddenly struck by a health problem that inspired me to eat only organic foods and eliminate meat, white sugar, white flour, and dairy from my diet. Well, it's just amazing how few restaurants serve brown rice or anything besides white bread, and of those restaurants that include lovely salads and vegetables, almost none are organic.

My interest in organic vegetables led me to health food stores. Having fresh foods on hand meant someone had to go shopping more than once a month. All of a sudden, the shopping duties were falling to me. . . . I was becoming a traditional female spouse despite myself—awk!!!

Help, now what was I supposed to do? Back to square one (and I don't mean Joyce Goldstein's restaurant, either). I'm going to have to teach John how to shop organically. *I've* learned. You just notice whether a carrot has a red sign or a blue sign over it. Red is good, it means organic. Blue is bad, it means conventionally grown with pesticides and chemical fertilizer, at least at Whole Foods in Mill Valley. At Wild Oats the colors are green for organic and orange for pesticides. But he can read. Then there are the bins, and teaching John what millet looks like—after I've just learned myself.

In the first four months of this arrangement, John hasn't complained once about missing grocery shopping. Initially it has been fun for me to "discover" all of these new foods that I'd never purchased before: millet, amaranth, shiitake mushrooms, sunflower sprouts, miso, kale, flaxseed oil, sea vegetables. But I sense that I may be reaching the point where it will become a "chore" again, like any other chore. A chore that I will want to share.

So here I am in the traditional woman's role of advocating good nutrition and healthy foods and doing all of the shopping. I have found a listing of vegetarian restaurants in the Bay Area, and now I'm in the process of locating the best of them. We'll have to drive instead of walk to most of them, but what's a few miles in search of an egalitarian lifestyle?

Meanwhile, I rack up hours of unpaid domestic labor, shopping and preparing whole foods—my delayed hippie phase. Some people have a late-life child; I'm having a late-life organic foods experience. I haven't figured out yet how to negotiate a trade for these developing domestic skills. I fantasize that John will be seized by some dormant domestic urge to prepare vegetarian meals. I pray to the Grocery Goddess that she will attract John to the new Wild Oats store on Chestnut Street. Sowing wild oats is a male thing, after all. Most likely we'll work something out piecemeal, and my list of good vegetarian restaurants will grow.

For now it feels like no good deed goes unpunished. I improve my diet and inherit a traditional woman's role that I'd escaped for years before and during married life. But then, I have lost 28 pounds.

RECOVERING FROM EXCELLENCE

Charli Depner

IT IS EASY TO SPOT a fellow junkie. "I can enter an unlimited number of activities in a single day," oozed a colleague, unmistakably high on his new electronic datebook. Infinite time. The ultimate seduction. People like me can't handle this stuff. My name is Charli Depner and I am recovering from excellence, an addiction first diagnosed in the 1980s and now sweeping the country in epidemic proportions. It begins innocently enough. I started out experimenting with personal mission statements, fooling around with distilling them into measurable goals. Before I knew it, I was saddled with a 22-item-per-day "To Do" list habit. I was running up debts at stationery and electronics counters, trying to satisfy an insatiable craving for the time management system that would let me have it all—and smugly tick off each item at the end of the day, just to prove it.

By the time I acknowledged that I had a problem, life had become a nightmarish succession of failed relationships with datebooks, organizers, and electronic gizmos. It got so bad at one point that I was two-timing my filofax for the sleazy little day runner at the office. The pattern was always the same. Sure, there was the honeymoon period of insatiable data transfers, but that soon gave way to the inevitable arguments over failures to perform. I'd be accused of demanding too much. What system could accommodate the impromptu staff meeting that bumps the conference call into my daughter's ballet lesson? My needs were not being met, but I would feel guilty about not putting enough into the relationship. In the end, it was always the same. We would give up trying to communicate and drift apart.

I decided to seek help. The first thing I had to confront was the irrational belief that one can "make time." No matter how clever we are, there are still only 24 hours in the day. I forced myself to do the math on the growing list of items on my personal development list; you know, those things that will turn your life around if you can "carve out" a mere 30 minutes a day to do them—things like Stairmaster, Spanish, morning pages, keeping a stock of peeled raw vegetables in the refrigerator. Well the thing is, the items on my list, if followed faithfully, added up to the equivalent of a full-time job—and, being a mom, I already have a couple of those.

That leads me to another common delusion—that any time management system is sophisticated enough to deal with a woman's life. Think about it. They make all the wrong assumptions. They expect you to do one thing at a time, as if you can't pack lunches while picking up voice-mail. They don't interface schedules for the simultaneous roles women are expected to perform, as if you don't squeeze in a few minutes at the company picnic before making an appearance at the charity fund-raiser scheduled at the same time. They ignore the routine need for alternative iterations of the entire calendar, as if there were no such things as babysitter no-shows, homework that falls out of the backpack, or head lice epidemics. They don't seem to recognize that a woman's life is shared with the people in it. She doesn't do everything alone. The schedule is contingent on others showing up—and, with any luck, not vomiting.

With these new insights, I began the process of recovering from excellence. I invite you to try the 12 steps of my program:

1. Admit that you are powerless. Life in the '90s no longer resembles an orderly sequence of activities stacked up neatly on a Gantt chart. It's more like the guy spinning plates on the *Ed Sullivan Show*.

2. Refuse to grease the squeaky wheel. Don't confuse the urgent stuff with the things that really matter.

3. Search for meaning beyond the bottom line. Entertain the radical notion that the process may be more precious than the outcome.

4. Generalize the First Rule of Housekeeping, "Everything worth doing is not worth doing well."

5. Balance is the key to a long, healthy life. If Peter is chronically robbed to pay Paul, sooner or later Peter will get pissed.

6. Celebrate your ability to make choices. You can't have it all and, even if you could, you really wouldn't want to have to take care of it all.

7. Refine your appreciation for the outrageous and the unanticipated. Get in touch with your powers of improvisation.

8. Learn to laugh about it.

9. Don't confuse taking care of yourself with flipping off the rest of the planet. Light a candle rather than curse the darkness; just don't burn it at both ends.

10. Regard time as the most precious commodity. Be choosy about the people you savor it with.

11. Develop a repertoire of cheap thrills. It doesn't take any extra time to use glitter crayons and scented markers. You get points for style.

12. Just say, "No!"

TOP OF THE HILL

Ronnie Caplane

THIS MORNING I JOGGED 3.75 miles, did 150 stomach crunches, 30 leg lifts, 50 arm extensions holding two-pound weights, and three and a half girls' push-ups.

Yesterday was my birthday. My 49th birthday. To celebrate I'm going to lose ten pounds, squeeze into my old size-8 bellbottom jeans, and grow my hair three inches below my shoulders.

Frankly I am shocked to be 49. I don't feel 49. I don't look 49. I'm not even sure what 49 feels like or what 49 looks like.

Forty-nine sounds so old. It's decades after 25 and only a hair from 50.

Forty-nine-year-olds don't jog 3.75 miles a day. They don't go to rock concerts and scream. They don't play dress-up with their dogs.

When my mother was 49 she was much older than I am. Her children had already graduated from college. One was a lawyer and the other was married. She went to the beauty shop every week, played bridge and said things like, "Is it hot in here or is it just me?"

My children aren't even out of high school. I don't play bridge and I know "it's just me."

But that was when 49 was middle-aged. Now there's age inflation. With adolescence lasting longer, women having children later, and people living longer they've changed the definition of middle age. Now it doesn't start until 55 or 58.

My friend Don says I'm in for a year of struggle, clinging by my fingernails to some of my youthful fantasies like being a ballerina, or flying across a stage like Mary Martin in *Peter Pan*, or squeezing into size-8 anything.

It's also a year when I'll dump other illusions like having another child, going to medical school, or expecting my hair to grow in dark brown like it used to.

He says it's a good experience and that 50 is a lot more relaxing than 49.

But what does he know. He's a guy.

Forty-nine is very confusing. I feel 25 and don't understand why the grocery store clerk calls me ma'am, offers to load the car, and never flirts with me. Or how my children's teachers got to be younger than I am. Or why the Civil Rights Movement is "history."

Sometimes, I catch my reflection in a store window and I don't recognize me. It's not the packaging I expect.

My friend Betsy put her finger on it. I really like the way I feel inside my body, she told me, I just don't like the way it looks from the outside.

She's right. There's a comfort that comes with age that was never there at 25. It's what allows me to take tap dancing and sing along with the radio even when someone else is in the car.

I read the obituaries every day and check out the age of the people who died. I no longer consider cosmetic surgery a cop-out and coloring my hair is as natural as brushing my teeth. Gray is gorgeous, but not on me.

Pulling out a penlight in a candle-lit restaurant to read the menu, or kicking several pieces of clothing into one pile so I only have to bend down once, or walking past a construction site and not having to endure the rude and intrusive catcalls of the workers, gets me mad.

But no age has been easy.

I cried all through my 30th birthday dinner because I was joining the generation of people you couldn't trust. Forty was no piece of cake. I think I grew my hair long that year too. It seemed unimaginably old until I was 41.

My father turned 80 last year and he said he doesn't understand how he got to be that old. To me, he's been old as long as I've known him but he doesn't feel that way.

I never really wanted to be a ballerina, and if I went to medical school now I'd qualify for a senior citizen discount before I completed all my training.

When I was 25 I probably wanted to lose ten pounds anyway.

But I'm not throwing out those size-8 Levis. At least not until I turn 50.

And that's years from now.

Appeared in Ronnie's "Under Construction" column in the *Alameda (CA) Journal*.

ON MY ALTAR

Suzanne LaFetra

FALL REMINDS ME that time is always moving. It is the time of year when the warm Indian summer hardens into the chilly crunch of early winter. It is a time when change flutters all around us, as the tomatoes and basil in the garden make way for squash and figs. Fall gently nudges me to feel my own mortality, and in doing so, it pushes me to celebrate my life. Feeling the season turn reminds me to drink up, enjoy what is here, right now.

Mexicans have mastered the ability to squeeze the fullness of life from the cold reality of death. On November 1st they celebrate Day of the Dead, lifting the delicate veil that separates the dead from the living. Graves are cleaned and adorned with flowers and candles. Altars are built, heavy with incense and *cempasúchitl*, the pungent marigold, the sweet acrid scents guiding the spirits back home. It is a scene awesome and bittersweet to observe, a day brimming with both life and death.

Day of the Dead honors those who have passed, but for me it also honors the passage of time itself. It demands that I pause, remember, grieve, celebrate, live fully. In savoring the past, and grieving for that which is gone, I clear a path for my future.

Each year, as October closes, I build my own altar. Last year as I scattered the orange petals across photos of my grandparents and a newspaper from September 10th, I was pregnant with my second child. This year, my family now complete, I balance my baby daughter in the crook of my arm as my son plays with a smiling sugar skull. I smooth the familiar embroidered cloth, and acknowledge my once-young self, this body that will never again grow a child. I trim marigold stems, thinking back on life before my children came—driving home at sunrise, wandering through Oaxaca buying old silver, lazing in bed on a Sunday with my husband. Lighting the incense, I wonder about the future: Will my daughter be a musician? Will my son ride horses? Will I ever hold a grandbaby? I fill my altar with golden flowers, the keys to a business I once owned, a picture of my round, pregnant belly. These symbols of my own milestones brighten as I light the candles. I breathe in my past, hold it—then let it go.

With young children, there is no ignoring the passing of time. It saunters along, as we buy new shoes (again!) and shake our heads at how those pants fit just fine last week. As my baby daughter sprouts into childhood, bittersweet pangs rumble as I pack away her now-too-small ruffly sundress and doll-sized diapers. I mourn a little when my two-year-old son stops requesting a lullaby each night before bed. I pause for a moment, savoring the scene: my daughter crawling toward my son, who zooms his toy train past her; they both erupt in giggles. Then I taste future memories—watching my son fly away without wobbly training wheels, hunting for meteors on a dark night with my teenagers in the high Sierras, rejoicing as a mortarboard is flung into the air.

I watch as my memories play back, a kaleidoscope of one thing becoming another. I entered adulthood on a Mexican adventure, which became a business in San Francisco selling folk art. I traded that business for motherhood and a home with a delicious garden in Berkeley. As my children grow I find myself ripening into a writer. The cycle continues, endings become beginnings. And today, as I pull the last tomatoes from their sprawling gangly vine, I look both back and ahead, feeling the turn of the clock.

As the days grow shorter, I bow to the passage of time. I am grateful for the fall harvest: magnificent squashes, warm, spicy soups, sensuous persimmons, dripping with juice. Savoring the delicacies of this brief season, knowing that they are ripe only for the moment, makes them that much richer. I want to drink fully, open-throated.

Winter approaches, the wheel keeps turning, my son learns to whistle, my daughter sleeps through the night. I find a gray hair, and smiling, set it aside for my altar next year.

WHERE DOES THE BOGEYMAN LIVE?

Kathleen Faraday & Joan Stevenson

KATHLEEN WRITES: My first experience with fear was waking up in the morning as a little girl and realizing that my ribbons had fallen out of my ringlets. I was certain that the bogeyman who I knew lived under the bed had snatched them.

My younger sister and I would repeatedly sneak quick peeks under the bed, squeal with our imagined terror, and race to the top of the stairs where we would bumpety-bump our way down on our bottoms. I see us flirt with our fears as we went door to door trick or treating. Ever skeptical of the witches and goblins, we were willing to face our fears to add more candy to our stash. We even braved our neighbor's spook house where someone looking very much like her father rose up out of a coffin and mumbled "EEEEH." We shrieked as we put our hands in a bowl of peeled grapes masquerading as cats' eyes.

As a child, my subconscious could turn anything into a nightmare and I had many. My parents always consulted the *Parents* magazine movie guide before allowing me to see a movie. Finally in my teens I was permitted to join my friends for the movie *Psycho* as part of our Halloween festivities. Well, I am here to tell you that 40 years later, I never take a shower without thinking of that film. I can't get the soap out of my eyes fast enough. I brought this up with the walking group this morning and Darcy said that she not only locks the bathroom door, but sometimes she sets the alarm system before showering for that very same reason.

So here we are in October 2001 and the bogeyman is out there blatantly tampering with our lives. Now my fears are more pervasive, more global, founded on fact. I am conscious of every move I make—wondering. . .

Shall I drink the water?

Shall I eat the bread?

Shall I go to the theater?

Shall I ride the BART?

Shall I take that plane?

Shall I open that mail?

I wish I knew that the bogeyman still lived only under my bed.

JOAN WRITES: Amanda grabbed my finger in her firm grip and with eyes that sparkled led me to her closet. Loosing my hand, she pointed up at the polka-dot clown outfit. At two she has caught the anticipation of her big sisters and, while not understanding Halloween, she knows it will be exciting.

The goblins that roamed the street when I was young had no elaborate costumes. Mother's white apron and a mop head turned me into Raggedy Ann. My sheet-shrouded brother as a ghost accompanied me. The first stop on Halloween was the house we all knew treated us to wonderful homemade popcorn balls.

Twenty years later, in Lafayette, my children climbed cautiously up the steep candlelit driveway to Ruth Ann's house where a scary witch with a cackling voice lifted goodies from a steaming cauldron while her husband, hidden behind a bush, banged on a tin pie plate.

Perhaps I sentimentalize, but that was the way I remember Halloween. Foolishly I took it for granted.

Terrorism is not new. It has crept stealthily into our culture. The sick neighbor who adds laxatives or razor blades to a child's candy is a terrorist. The shadowy predator who threatens our children as they walk to school is a terrorist. The faceless pedophile who engages a lonely teenager in a chat room is a terrorist. They have robbed us of our freedom and they have stolen a precious part of childhood.

And so Katie and Meghan (the princess and Britney Spears) will take their little sister, the clown, to trick or treat in a well-lit mall. All candy will be hermetically sealed and the merchants will write off the entire cost as a business expense. We will continue to drive our children to the schoolyard, despite the cost, the traffic, and the pollution. We will call on Norton Utilities Family Security to monitor our family Internet access.

Freedom? Maybe we have been waving it goodbye for longer than we realize.

Appeared October 24, 2001 in Kathleen and Joan's column "Double Talk" in the *Contra Costa (CA) Sun.*

THE ROOTS OF TERRORISM

Gina Waldman

THIRTY-FOUR YEARS AGO my family and I narrowly escaped death by a terrorist attack in Tripoli, Libya. It was 1967; I was 19 years old at the time. A group of terrorists attempted to burn the bus, which was taking us to the airport, while we were desperately fleeing the country. With the recent events that have scarred our nation, my own personal scar has been reopened by the memories of my past.

In the last weeks Americans have been saturated by media reports showing hundreds of young children "studying" in religious schools in Pakistan and Afghanistan, and we know the same thing is taking place in the West Bank and Gaza. We also know, thanks to the comprehensive coverage of the media, that these children are taught rejection of the modern world, hatred and resentment of the American way of life and the Judeo-Christian ethics; we are considered "infidels." The philosophy of these *Madrasas*—religious schools—is simple: if you are not with us, you must be against us. Years of brainwashing and propaganda deliver, ready and willing, *Jihad*—holy war—soldiers to be trained as suicide bombers.

Individual freedom, democracy, and equality, especially fundamental human rights for women, are a grave threat to most Muslim nations. Cultural resentment is easily turned into anti-Western rage and a rejection of modern and progressive countries exemplified by Western values. Diversity is not cherished or tolerated in countries like

Pakistan, Afghanistan, Iran, Saudi Arabia, or Libya. This ideology has not changed at all since I was forced to flee Libya over 30 years ago; in fact, in some instances, the restrictions on women have worsened. Women are forced into complete segregation, are not permitted to get an education, and are their husbands' property.

As a Westerner, and most of all, as a woman who grew up in an oppressive environment, I firmly believe that it is high time these Muslim religious schools radically change their philosophy and teach the true original values of the Koran: to love and care for other human beings, regardless of their race, religion, or creed. Some *Mullahs*—religious leaders—have used and continue to use these very schools as conduits to plant the seeds that grow the roots for future terrorist movements.

By propagating hatred against us "infidels," they will cultivate willing subjects to sacrifice as the next suicide bomber to fight their own wars.

When I watch the news, I see these children being indoctrinated from early childhood. I ponder their faces and ask myself: "Which one of these children will be given the 'honor' to die for *Jihad*?"

Our government is mistaken in thinking that getting rid of the Taliban will eradicate terrorism. The hundreds of children that are being indoctrinated as we bomb the Taliban will soon rise and hit us again. Only by then, they will have an even more passionate cause for revenge: they will honor their fathers and the Taliban's memories in the name of *Jihad*.

Part of our responsibility is to join in with the Muslim communities worldwide in honoring the values of the Koran. It is my hope that Muslim leaders will take a closer look at the *Madrasas* and reevaluate the teachings that take place there. True Muslims should insist on teaching the values of compassion and love, not inflame the children's hearts and minds against the *kafirs*—infidels.

Appeared November 6, 2001 in the *Marin (CA) Independent Journal.*

LOOKING FOR ME

LOOKING FOR ME:
Haiku of a Suburban Mother

Susan Antolin

blinded, as if stepping out
of a darkened theater
is this my life?

your shoes in my way
all I have of you
this long day

your disgust
at rotting produce in the fridge
do I know you?

spiral notebook
among scattered mail
idle, patient

if I never write
will the illusion that I can
last forever?

cheap potted plant
bought for green foliage
unexpectedly blooms

cradled in pounding rhythms
for one moment
I find the old me

"urban ambiance"
as host closes out city noise
our parched souls drink it in

radio at full volume
foot on the gas
writing again!

happy, even in line
at the post office
wearing new shoes

driving the rental van
on a made-up errand
freedom for an hour

flowing lines
scribbled at night
in the light of the bathroom

the baby in her own bed
for one night
larger hands reach for me

even drained of milk
my breast
comforts her to sleep

tiny hands caress
my skin
willing more milk to come

roses passed over the fence
warm sunshine on our faces
kind neighbors

fashionably late
lone daisy rises from autumn leaves
in quiet solitude

clear blue autumn sky
in mother's 65th year
a new romance

after months of illness
head thrown back
with laughter

hands in soapy water
I smile, alone
Mom is in love!

sharing secrets
like sisters
divorced Mom and I

what are the odds:
a child's aimless swing of the net
catches a Monarch

flawless hair and nails
suburban costume
not my size

mindless of kids' chatter
and changed traffic light
lost in memories

even from my six-year-old
"you are beautiful"
makes me pause mid-thought

to settle the question
of whether to keep him home
our son throws up

children raised
without slightest deprivation
whine with boredom

like lowering the volume
on a radio
my son tunes me out

child molesters, snipers, terrorists
a sleeping child rolls over
unaware

complete love in your eyes
yet not old enough to carry a memory
beyond this year

days packed with activity
empty, save for a few moments
alone writing

telephone in hand
words rehearsed silently for years
remain unspoken

stroke of genius!
I throw unmatched socks
in the trash

forty-nine-cent spiral notebook
thirty-two-cent pen
therapy on the cheap

precariously
tall and leaning stack of words
my bedside reading

a haiku poem
inadvertently written
in five-seven-five

jeans with tattered holes
won't even let me pretend
I am young again

dog sprawled on sunny floor
in the eye of a stormy day
wall clock ticks

my lap finally free
the dog ambles away
to the other couch

extra meat in your dish
any easier to bear
this quiet day?

grasshopper alone
on our stairway wall
he and I lost in Walnut Creek

what comfort?
watching fish swim circles
trapped in fish bowl

the earth curves
and continues
beyond this town

SUNDAY WRITER

Martha C. Slavin

I WAS RAISED BY an artistic family. Both of my parents were professional artists, my grandfather was a professional photographer, and I have numerous cousins who work in the art world. My family looked with a measure of disdain upon Sunday painters. Before I was in grade school, I was encouraged to draw and paint and to consider myself an artist. All the way through high school, I was called the artist of the school, the one everyone turned to for posters, event program covers, drawings, and dance decorations.

When I went away to college and art school, I would walk around the art room looking at everyone's work in progress and realize that I was one of the more skilled students there. But I also began to realize that I did not have the passion for art. I didn't think about drawing and painting, nor did I practice it regularly beyond the classroom. My father could draw from memory a dog running and make every hair on his body bristle with joy. When I drew, I never could get beyond the slightly stilted poses, the minor errors in composition or color placement that would transform me from an art student into the ranks of the professional artist.

Knowing that to be an artist I needed to perfect my skills, I allowed my roaring inner critic to defeat me. I gave up drawing and painting. At first, I just put away my instruments and sealed my drawings into portfolios. I have made a still life of my brushes and paint palettes.

These actions may seem defeatist, but I don't miss drawing at all, and I have taken my art education and used it in other more satisfying ways. I have taught art to many students, and I have encouraged my own son to explore his creativity.

I come from a completely different perspective to writing. No one in my family had seriously considered being a writer, therefore I have no one's example to follow. I look at myself as a beginner. I have learned to talk back to my inner critic and say, "I'm just learning, I'm just beginning, this is the best I can do right now, I'm not going to publish this anyway, this is practice."

One of the first pieces that I wrote concerned an eccentric neighbor of ours while I was growing up. The first time I wrote about her, I merely wrote a short paragraph describing her and her house. Her story evolved into a fictionalized account about the tension between her, a mother, and a daughter.

With this story as with others that I have since written, I find that I can use my inner critic. After the mad thrall of creating, I can step away from my writing and let my inner critic read it with an objective eye. He will say, "Oh," in a flat voice, "is this all there is?" I've learned to say back, "But I am still learning. You're right. It needs this and this and this. This is not a perfect piece, but look how much better it is than last year's writing. This year I can make it into a story. Just wait. It will come."

When I was training to be an artist, I would have been satisfied only if I could attain the greatness of a Milton Glaser, or a Paul Rand, both in graphic arts, or a Rembrandt, in fine art. I was not willing to accept anything less, but I wasn't willing to work hard enough to reach that kind of goal. I expected my skill to just be there; after all, I was the artist.

In my writing, I am giving myself time, time to explore what I am capable of doing. Though I know I am not pushing myself enough and I may never be a published author, I don't care at the moment. I am more interested in following the path that my writing is opening up to me. By writing in a journal, I have been able to resolve many personal conflicts. By practicing personal essays, I have learned to understand and present my own opinions more clearly. By writing fiction, I have tested my creativity. Perhaps I will always be a Sunday writer, but what I am learning is filling my life up with new understanding and awareness.

A NEW COUNTRY

Carole Sirulnick

IT IS HARD TO BELIEVE that just a few weeks ago I was relaxed and traveling, that I had the time and inclination to leisurely comment on those around me, and that now, some moments of my life feel like that irritating CNN newscast. How would my headlines read?

Well, today I choreographed the ins and outs of two painters, an electrician, a cabinetmaker with seven patient hours. In between, I walked a brisk two miles (the weather is springlike and glorious) and Xeroxed a thousand mailing labels for the May workshop.

During a ten-minute break, I also spoke with a dour woman who is available to officiate at my wedding. My wedding???!! Yes, I am getting married, or as my nine-year-old says, "You have a fiancé— that is French, Mommy." She earnestly asks, "What will change?" I say to her with much determination, "Not much, honey." But inside I know everything will change. My life and my sense of space and territory. My self definition. My future and the present. And of course, our family.

Certainly I have shifted already, for in order to consider another marriage, I've had to move on from my stance that I would never marry again. But what have I altered? Rearranged? Or is it that I've expanded?

One week, I was an unmarried, divorced, single woman with a so-called boyfriend of six years. Now I am calling caterers, looking at wedding rings, and juggling the requests of many others regarding my wedding. Not theirs, mind you.

I guess it is like a wonderful traveling experience for I've discovered that I am not the same person I thought I was. In the past six years, I have journeyed from wanting a lover—to needing a more conventional structure. I have walked along and slowly crossed borders into familiar yet new lands. Yes, I've been married before, but that was then. And now—I can define it anew. A clean passport, a new photo, a new marital status.

From the class journal.

LAWYER MOM

Ronnie Caplane

I STARED AT THE CHECKOUT CLERK over bags overflowing with Fig Newtons, glass cleaner, Cheerios, fruit rollups, milk, English muffins, and toilet paper.

"Work number?" he repeated, pen poised over my check.

My whole being, my very definition of self was reduced to two words—Work Number.

I used to have a work number.

Should I explain that I'm a lawyer? That I quit the practice to stay home with my children? That I would have another work number. Someday. Soon. In a year, or two.

Would he refuse my check? Post my name on every cash register, branding me as "A woman without a Work Number"? Make me return the groceries to the shelf?

I did the only honorable thing I could.

I lied. Brazenly I recited my husband's office number.

Three weeks before I was a briefcase-toting, high-heeled, dress-for-success trial attorney. Another person in another life who wasn't cowed by a grocery clerk's request for a work number.

I used to have contempt for women like me.

Women who abandoned their careers to stay home and raise children. Women who didn't have power lunches, secretaries, or electronic pocket organizers. Dull, boring, cooing, Cheerio-buying, I-work-in-the-home women.

I signed on for the Gloria Steinem you-can-have-it-all plan. Short labor, natural childbirth, Willie Nelson singing backup, and home in 48 hours. In two months I'd be bored, slim, and back at work.

I was ordered, organized, and on top of it all.

Then I had the baby.

I started talking nonsense in falsetto. I bonded. I cooed. I watched my baby nap and cried at the thought of college in 18 years. Questions of breast versus bottle and cloth versus disposal were more engaging than sovereign immunity, discretionary function, or even *res judicata*.

I returned to work with baby on the brain.

Two and a half years later there was a second baby and life, as we knew it, came to an end. Weekends and evenings became a blur of vacuuming, cleaning, and trips to the supermarket.

Quality time was a myth created by the childless.

Having it all was more than I could handle and spending nine or ten hours at the office everyday hadn't gotten any easier.

One night between shoveling laundry and scraping crusted macaroni off the wall my husband suggested that I quit practicing law for a while and stay home with the children.

I was outraged. What about my education? What about my clients? What about being a good role model? If I could get by on two hours of sleep a night, I could manage it all.

How dare he make such a suggestion? If I weren't so exhausted I'd demand a divorce.

But the seed was planted. I imagined food in the refrigerator all the time. Taking the children to the doctor when they were sick rather than forcing them to "act well" until Saturday rolled around. To drive on a field trip and not lie to my boss.

I took the plunge and three months later I was out of the practice of law.

At first I was adrift without the daily structure of depositions, court appearances, and stacks of phone calls to return. But a whole new set of activities quickly filled my schedule—carpools, fund-raisers, classroom volunteering.

I negotiated, mediated, and resolved disputes but the issues were bedtime stories, washing dishes, and who gets to sleep with the dog. Coordinating three carpools, eight children, snacks, baseball games, orthodontic appointments, and horseback-riding lessons is as challenging as any complex litigation.

A law school classmate becoming a partner in a prestigious firm, judge, or head of some agency brings out the green monster in me. It's the old road-not-taken thing.

But the practice of law will always be there and these years with my children are transitory. They can't be reclaimed. I miss business trips, the rush of a well-executed cross-examination, and the respect that comes with being a lawyer. But the road I've been on for the past decade has made a difference to the most important people in my life.

I don't even care what checkout clerks think when I say I don't have a work number. They take my check anyway.

Appeared in Ronnie's "Under Construction" column in the *Alameda (CA) Journal*.

THE MUSIC MAN

Linda Joy Myers

THE DAY BEGINS AS USUAL in Mrs. Rockwell's fourth-grade class—the Pledge of Allegiance, the Lord's Prayer, and a round of spelling. Outside the classroom, we hear a flurry of activity. Melodious phrases of music waft into the room from the hall. A tall, willowy man with bright red hair tumbling over his forehead appears, a violin tucked under his chin. He dips and sways as he enters the doorway, his enchanting sounds making us stop what we are doing. He amazes us with his graceful movements. His violin sings melodies from heaven. We leave our seats to gather around him and drink in the magic. He kneels to our level, grinning, his blue eyes shining, and winks as he unfurls "Turkey in the Straw," then some melody that makes me think of clouds and God. My chest hurts. I want more than anything to draw such sweet sounds into the world.

"Hey folks, this is called a violin. It is one of the stringed instruments in the orchestra. How many of you want to play an instrument?" I am hypnotized by his violin. It speaks in high notes and low, sultry tones, silky and intimate; it laughs and tells jokes. His bow flies into the air and comes back down on the right string. White stuff called rosin flies all over.

"My name is Mr. Brauninger, the orchestra teacher. Do any of you want to join our orchestra? You could play the violin and any other of our stringed instruments. You just have to take a slip home to your parents to be signed."

I come to him, drawn to his warmth and bright eyes. To his golden-toned violin. He asks me my name.

"Linda Joy."

"Linda Joy. What a pretty name you have, Linda Joy." He is looking directly into my eyes. I feel more important than I have ever felt in my whole life. He looks at me as if I'm a real person and talks to me as if what I say matters to him. He gives me a permission slip and tells me that I have to get my parents to sign it if I want to come to the orchestra next week.

"I don't have parents. I live with my grandmother."

He doesn't seem to think there's something wrong with me because I live with my grandmother, but I know I'm the only kid whose parents are divorced. I'm sure none of their parents fight like my mother does with my grandmother when she comes once a year on the train. Mr. Brauninger's smile makes all that go away.

He plays a jig that sets toes to tapping, but Mrs. Rockwell tells us to sit down in our seats and fold our hands like polite children. Mr. Brauninger plays something soft and sweet, his face tender with the music, his lips quivering when he reaches for the high notes. The fingers of his left hand vibrate back and forth. I want to cry. I could sit at his feet all day. I have to be included in his orchestra. I begin to scheme and plan what I can say to persuade my grandmother.

When I go home that afternoon, the determination to play the violin rides in solid clarity in my chest. I will do whatever it takes to be with the man with red hair, with the emanations of love that flow from him in waves. I tell Gram about the man who came to class with the wonderful violin. I promise her that I'll practice, she won't have to remind me.

"Please, please, please let me play the violin."

She nods and takes a drag on her cigarette. The room is filled with smoke. I see from her eyes that I need to let her think about it.

I know she wants me to be a famous musician. I convince her that the violin is what I am meant to play. Later that evening, I promise not to neglect my hour of piano practicing each day, and to finish all my music theory assignments.

I hear her talk to him on the phone after I go to bed. The next morning I find out that they decided that I should play the cello instead of the violin. Gram tells me, "You'll be more popular, there's less competition."

I am disappointed. I want to play the violin, but she says that there is a cello waiting for me.

I'll play anything just to be near him.

THE FIRST DAY OF ORCHESTRA is on Thursday of the next week. My shoes squeak as I walk on the polished walnut-colored cork floors and down the stairs to the basement music room. It is raining outside. The school smells of oil, wood, and musty dust in the thick curtains of the windows. Mr. Brauninger greets me with the same smile and shakes my hand again. An irrepressible happiness fills me up. He shows us the stringed instruments.

"This is a violin. Next to it is a viola, a little bigger." He plays a few notes to demonstrate the deeper range of the viola. He picks up a cello.

"Linda Joy, I talked to your grandmother and we thought maybe the cello would be best for you. It's a special instrument for a special girl like you. I picked out one just your size." He holds up a burnished brown cello, half-sized to fit me.

He shows us how the stringed instruments are constructed, the curves of the ribs, how the maple comes together in the back of the instrument to make a beautiful wavy pattern with a perfect seam. The intricately carved bridge, the nut at the top of the fingerboard, ebony pegs to tune the instrument, the graceful scroll, and strings made of steel and catgut. Curlicue F-holes carved in the top allow the sound to emerge from the belly. The sound post connects the top with the back, creating a vibration in the instrument. The bow is made of pernambuco wood from Brazil. Horsehair from real horses is strung from an ivory tip covered all the way to the ebony part where we hold the bow, called the frog.

"Ribbet, ribbet," he says, grinning, his eyes shining as he looks at each of us. He shows us how to drape our hands over the frog. We take turns holding the bow, learning to place it on the string, how to pull it smoothly. I watch the string widen as it vibrates. When I put my fingers on the ebony fingerboard, I can feel the hardness of the string under each finger pad. It hurts my tender fingers, but I am making music. I am playing the cello.

MR. BRAUNINGER BECOMES MY GUIDE and inspiration into realms of beauty. I suppose I fall in love with him. I practice often because I want Mr. Brauninger's face to light up. He draws little pictures in my string book to make me laugh—little men whose noses lie over the edge of the lines and spaces—but it is the look on his face that sustains me. He sees the music in me and coaxes it from me. He helps me find something greater than the disharmony at home; he is my guide to find the true harmony that lives inside me.

I become "the girl with the cello," part of the "strange" musician kids. The next stage of development is the Youth Orchestra on Saturday mornings. The best musicians in Owema are selected to play real music, "symphonic literature," as Mr. Brauninger calls it.

The first time I am supposed to go, I am nervous. The night before, I polish my cello and Gram rolls my hair so it would be fluffy. She is particularly happy because she believes I have "talent." Mr. Brauninger told her so. They talk about Carnegie Hall, but I don't know what she means. It seems like a foreign, scary world, but because of Mr. Brauninger, anything I could imagine with my cello is possible.

The Youth Orchestra meets in the basement of the high school music room. The building is huge, and the halls long. I can't imagine ever being old or big enough for high school. I find that I am one of the smallest children in the room. My natural shyness makes me want to hide, but I put on a brave face. I need to go meet the other string kids standing around with their instruments.

A clump of kids gathers around Mr. Brauninger. Mr. B. is the tall one, his red hair a beacon in the middle of the room. Already the French horns, trumpets, and woodwinds are tuning up, sitting in the upper levels of the tiered room. The noise is huge and thrilling. I try to conquer my shyness as I wander over to the group of kids around Mr. B. A boy with jet-black hair is laughing in a deep voice, his voice already changed, obviously older. He turns toward me, soft-brown eyes behind black horn-rimmed glasses, hands fiddling with change in his pockets. "There she is, the new girl."

Mr. Brauninger introduces me. "This is Keith. He's first chair cello, a wonderful cellist. This is Linda Joy."

"Nice to meet you, Linda Joy." Keith's dark eyes are like lassos, drawing me to him. He shakes my hand as if I'm an adult. He leans over to me and whispers in a conspiratorial voice, "Don't worry, you'll get the hang of things. It's nice you could join us. We've heard good things about you."

I am shocked to be already known. The group turns their faces toward me. I stand still, unsure of what to do next. Mr. Brauninger comes over, takes my cello, and puts his arm around me. "This is Linda Joy, a bright new star from Adams Grade School."

Another young girl with long dark hair flowing down her back, holding a cello, flashes me a quick smile. She is tall for her age, nearly as tall as Keith. Mr. Brauninger puts his hand on her shoulder. "This is Jodie from Emerson Grade School, another bright star. Do you know that you two started cello the same week last year?" There are murmurs and nods.

Next, I am introduced to redheaded twin boys who look alike except for their haircuts.

"This is Floyd, he plays the viola, and this is Lloyd, the violin. They're from Emerson School, too, and fine musicians."

They nod at me, and grin. "You can remember us this way— Floyd, flat top, Lloyd, long hair."

Jodie and I are the last two chairs in the cello section. Mr. Brauninger taps his baton softly, but the instruments blare on, trumpets, clarinets, oboes, and strings still a discordant blare. Then he bangs the baton against the metal stand on the podium and all the musicians put down their instruments.

"Good morning. We are here to play the greatest works of music ever written. This is the start of something new—a Youth Orchestra for all you talented musicians in town. Let me introduce you to the players you don't know, and then we'll get started with some Vivaldi, Bach, and a little Mozart. Some of you will not keep up with all the notes, but just do the best you can. Let's have fun."

The music builds up around me, filling the room with melodious sounds. Often the strings are out of tune, and the woodwinds squawk. The music rushes at us like a mountain stream. Jodie and I scrub away at our posts, watching Keith and the other cellists up front play with aplomb. I wonder if I'll ever be able to play like they do. At one point during a rest, Keith looks back and winks. Tingles rush up and down my body. He would never know from my smile how he affects me. He turns toward the front and leads the cello section all morning.

During Vivaldi's *Four Seasons*, thousands of notes rush by unplayed. Jodie and I look at each other helplessly, knowing that we both missed most of the notes, but I've never had so much fun in my life. Mr. Brauninger stops to demonstrate dynamics, how to crescendo and diminuendo, his fingers opening wide and then coming together like the hieroglyphs on the page. He tells jokes and stories about the composers, and makes wavy pictures with his hands to show how sound vibrates in the air and through the wood of our instruments. He helps us notice our poor intonation, which is rampant, and singles out each section to play separate passages, teaching us to hear how each person is playing and how the section works as one. We learn that we are one body of music-makers, no longer individuals. We must play together, feel together, and listen as one being to the composer's ideas coming alive in our time, through us.

The music rises above us, lifting us to a higher plane of knowledge, a realm of experience untouched by the rest of life. There is a beauty in the world that has no words, and a connectedness I could never imagine. It soothes the place within me that's sore from the absence of my mother and father.

Each week I am transported into this nether realm. The music is more than words, or ideas, or anything the mind could conceive of. It goes straight to my heart beating under my breastbone where my cello rests.

Excerpted from a memoir entitled *Don't Call Me Mother.*

LISTEN TO THE SILENCE

Michelle Wells Grant

"I WANT Y'ALL TO GO AWAY," said Mary, my neighbor from Louisiana, in response to her husband's question. "I want y'all to go away for two weeks so I can finish all the projects I've started." She was joking with him, of course, when he asked her what she wanted to do for a vacation this year.

She told me about this one spring day as we chatted on my porch, watching our children tear up and down the sidewalk on bikes and skateboards and wagons. We hooted. Wouldn't that be something? Two weeks alone in your own house. Free from laundry, cooking, bickering, noise. What would you do? The possibilities were too delicious to think about. We tried to remember if we had ever been totally alone in our own houses for more than a day since we'd had kids. Never. We fantasized. Nah, it would never happen. Nice idea though, Mary.

And boy, I didn't know anyone else who could use a reprieve from domestic life more than Mary. She is the mother of four boys and I was well aware of the demands her active household made on her. I, on the other hand, have only one child, my Elizabeth, just four then. I knew to what degree I devoted my life to my small family, but quadruple it! Geez.

More than amused by Mary's tangy reply to the vacation question, I told my husband, Mike, about it over dinner.

"And then she said, 'I want y'all to go away.'" I delivered it like a punch line to a joke.

"Ha!" he laughed. "Every mother's fantasy, I bet."

"No doubt."

Mike returned to his Mexican rice. Minutes later he put down his fork and said, "You know, we could do that."

I looked up. "Do what?"

"We could do that. Elizabeth and I could go somewhere for about a week, take a little vacation together, and let you have some time alone."

I nearly choked on my taco. "Yeah!" Elizabeth cheered. Was he serious? Yes, he was. Indeed, he was. It was one of those moments I shall never forget. He was offering me a wonderful gift. He offered it because he loves me.

And so it happened that I swiped Mary's fantasy, and although it had not been intentional, I felt a little sheepish about it when I told her. "Y'all go for it!" she said.

Mike and Elizabeth made plans to visit his parents in Southern California, their Daddy/Daughter Adventure they would call it. He looked forward to this time they would spend together, the kind of time I had with Elizabeth that he so often envied. I began to lay my plans. I made a laundry list of things I wanted to do during my week alone: work on my quilt, read, draw, clean out closets, write that children's story, rent a video or two, reorganize files, shop for a 20-year high school reunion dress, and more. It was an ambitious list. But the one thought that I secretly relished with anticipation and greed, like a squirrel with a nut, was the solitude. I have always loved being alone, entertaining myself through varied creative interests. I had known so little solitude since Elizabeth's birth and I yearned for a good dose of it. When they returned I would be rested and organized, satisfied with my stretch of solitude, content with my accomplishments. I would have a leg up on life.

Yet as the week approached I had doubts and mixed emotions. Would I miss them too much to enjoy my plans? Would I pine away without them? Is this what mommies should do? Some of my friends and relatives didn't think so. "Do you really want to send your family away for a week?" they asked, appalled. "Sure," I replied, confused by their response. What mother wouldn't? But while some were horrified that I might find this week-long separation from my family refreshing, others applauded it with envy. I resolved to suffer through the peace and quiet.

Finally, one Saturday morning, equipped with duffel bags, juice boxes, granola bars, Disney books on tape, and too many stuffed animals, Mike and Elizabeth were ready to hit the trail. I buckled Elizabeth into the seat and snuggled her animals around her. I stroked her silken hair and kissed her tender cheeks. I dutifully delivered my motherly parting instructions. ("Mind your Daddy, and don't trash Grandma and Grandpa's house.") Mike and I held our hug. "This will be good for all of us," he said. Yes, of course it would be. I knew that.

With moist eyes and a lump in my throat the size of a ping-pong ball, I watched Elizabeth blow me kisses until the car disappeared around the corner. Crumbling, I returned them. Now why did she have to do that? I turned and shambled up the porch steps. Inside, I saw the books I had set aside to read, stacked next to my comfortable chair. I saw the easel leaning in the corner, waiting to be assembled, the half-finished quilt on the table. I heard the silence. I felt the calm. "Yes!" I hissed, wiping the tears from my cheeks. "Yes!" The world was my oyster!

Of course I had to do one final pick-up before I could settle down; assorted toys, stray crayons and Barbie clothes, shoes and dirty socks, newspapers strewn hither and yon, wet bath towels on beds, neckties and half-empty soda cans. Amazingly, this paraphernalia once returned to its proper place was to stay there throughout the week. In the days ahead, I was to stare dumbly at the neat row of baby dolls on Elizabeth's bed, staring blankly back at me, or the tidy stack of Mike's *Car and Driver* magazines on the den table. "Whoa," I whispered in wonderment, "they're still there!"

Still, I could not settle down to read or sew. The bulging closets screamed at me, the laundry glared. I sorted mounds of outgrown clothes. I did two loads of laundry and folded what was to be the last of tiny socks and boxer shorts for that week. I tossed out broken toys. I changed sheets. I avoided my ambitious project list which sat on the kitchen counter waiting to be tackled.

I was disoriented those first two days. My normally active household, with neighborhood children in and out and televisions blaring, was silent as a tomb. But slowly, slowly the unfamiliarity eased and I turned the tomb into my own private spa.

I gave myself a manicure. I did my work-out tape. I brought my mail order catalogs into the bathroom and took long bubble baths, shopping as I soaked. From the tub, I saw my one lonely towel hanging on the rack. Some nights I went to bed early and got up at dawn to read or meditate. I noticed how the pure, iridescent morning light filtered through the shutters. Some nights I stayed up late and slept late in the morning, stretching in the spacious bed as I awoke, the sheets unusually cool. I made only one bed. I lingered over morning coffee, flipping through my stack of three months of virgin magazines. Outside the kitchen window, I watched the birds fight for a turn at the feeder.

And on my kitchen table, where normally I stand forever sorting socks and folding tiny clothes, I set up a still life of strawberries, tomatoes, and green beans from my garden, tumbled across a colorful dishtowel. I sketched it in pastels and called it "Mommy's Yield."

I ran my few errands efficiently and at top speed, without my dawdling partner in tow. No little pixie in the seat next to me whistling "It's a Small World" with that puckered-up rosebud of a mouth. No tender thigh to reach over and pat to the tune.

Mary waved from across the yard. "How's it going?" she called.

"Great! Real good! House sure is quiet. Come on over, hide out for a while," I shouted back.

"They'd find me, believe me," she laughed.

Evenings, normally all-consuming as every mother knows, were endless and leisurely. I did not beg Elizabeth to get into the bath, or prod her to brush her teeth, or nag her to pick up her room, or plead with her to get into bed. Instead, I watched a Tom Cruise video, read or cross-stitched. At times I did nothing.

I padded barefoot through my house, fearless and free of the land mines of spiked Barbie shoes. As I walked I fought the urge to swoop up the toys and clothes from the floor that were not there. It is a stride I have perfected over time, either a swooping, grasping motion like a pelican's dive for fish, or a storklike bobbing, dipping gait. The pelican dive is generally used for scooping up larger items such as dolls or shoes. The stork dip, however, is a sudden halt before a cluster of smaller items such as Lego pieces or the remains of an abandoned bag of potato chips. There is a bend at the waist, the pieces are gathered, and there are several Olympic strides before the next cluster is encountered. Again, the dip, and so on. This easy, upright gait across my uncluttered floor was foreign to me.

No short-order cooking for me this week. No way. I ate yogurt and salads, had pizza delivered. My stove collected dust, my dishwasher rarely ran. Dinner was leisurely and peaceful. No prodding a four-year-old to take at least one bite of the chicken. No attempts at dinner conversation with Mike, disrupted by a child with five pitted olives on the fingertips and "see" food in the gaping mouth. One plate to wash, one coffee cup. No ice cream cones to scoop.

By Thursday I had come to realize that I would not accomplish all that I had hoped to during my week alone. If only I had more time, I thought. But that wasn't it, I didn't need more time. I lacked momentum. Oh, I tackled the files and scribbled the beginnings of the children's book. Here and there I ticked off items on the list, but it seemed I had little motivation. I could not concentrate. I puttered and wasted precious time. And then I recognized the problem. I realized that my family paced me, that stolen time, snatched between the demands of domesticity, was far more productive than scheduled blocks of time. It was the limits on my time that fueled me, provided me with momentum. If I seemed to be at loose ends without my family now, I believe it was because the tether that normally paced me had slackened.

That evening I settled down with a good book and a favorite meal of grilled swordfish, salad, and French bread. Perhaps it was this particular time at the end of the day that did me in, when I regularly insist we all come together at the family table. I was halfway through that dinner when I felt the hole, the emptiness, the loneliness wash over me. My novel rested on the table, face down. My face fell to my open hands. My appetite, usually ravenous, was gone. I missed them terribly.

It was then I sat and wondered if I was really whole without them. Had I abandoned myself in my devotion to them? Am I but an appendage of them, sustained, in large part, by their love and need for me? How complete am I on my own? The thought crept into my mind (perhaps the forbidden thought that plays across every wife and mother's mind from time to time), what might become of me if I somehow tragically lost them? Would there be enough of me left over to continue on with life? These mournful thoughts were too much for me. I went to bed.

The next day I went to Mary's open house given in honor of her oldest son's high school graduation. Despite my intentions to lay low this week, I was grateful for the chance to mingle with friends and neighbors, to divert my focus.

"Well, how's it going?" Mary asked.

"They come home tomorrow," I said, grinning.

"Are you ready?" she said.

"I think so."

On Saturday I was as nervous as a schoolgirl getting ready for the prom. I set my hair on hot rollers, carefully applied makeup, and chose a pretty summer dress I had not worn in ages. I popped over to the market to pick up steaks for a welcome-home dinner. The butcher, who is accustomed to seeing me race through in khaki shorts and T-shirts, raised his eyebrows at this different look. Bet he thought I had a date.

I put away my quilt, my easel, my books. I prepared myself for the onslaught of laundry they would bring me, the duffel bags, cooler, and stuffed animals I knew they would dump on the dining room floor, that magnetic field for clutter. I thought about the things I had pushed from my mind a few nights before, the question that had loomed so frightfully. Was I complete without them? I decided it had been loneliness I had felt, nothing more. It was the rhythm of our lives together, the heartbeat of my family that I missed. Without them, it is my own heartbeat that I hear. I was not incomplete without them, I had not relinquished my identity to them. If I had lost anything over the past few years, it was my familiarity with myself. Perhaps I felt a stranger in my skin. This week, this mixed bag of emotions—the pleasure in my solitude mingled with the anguish of my loneliness—had been a somewhat jarring effort to get reacquainted with myself. Amazing what a mom can hear when she has the chance to listen to the silence.

The dusty car pulled in the driveway and the ping-pong ball came back to my throat. I held their sweaty, tired bodies close to my perfumed and rested one and felt the familiar pulse return as if it had never missed a beat. Our old routine snapped back to normal and became the sustenance of our lives as before, as expected. An hour later, I had dusted off my stove, fired up the washing machine, and shifted into my pickup stride.

That was three years ago. We did it again last year and I'm waiting for my week this year, waiting eagerly, I might add. Mary? Still waiting. As long as Mike and Elizabeth enjoy the Daddy/Daughter Adventure, I will gratefully accept the gift of a week alone. It takes some getting used to but I believe there is a place for a wife and mother's indulgence in solitude. I believe there is even a place for the ache that comes with it. I was a little wiser last year, prepared for that tug that their absence would have on me. I knew that there would be times when I would do little more than twiddle my thumbs because I missed them. That's okay. Knowing that, I may still say, "I want y'all to go away." That's okay too.

Appeared May 1996 in *Parents' Press* (Bay Area).

HOME TO RŮŽENA

Terri Hinte

IT'S ALMOST TIME TO PULL ANCHOR again: in just over six weeks, mother and I are heading for Bohemia and the home villages of her paternal grandparents. It always seemed a fabled place to me, not because of its castles and spas but because it was the birthplace of Růžena, the only great-grandparent I ever knew.

Families are funny: it's as much the *idea* of them that sustains as the actual hugs, or room and board. I was born the second of Růžena's nearly 40 great-grandchildren, and we knew we were her crowning achievement, the jewel-like cluster of stars around her head, as the venerated Our Lady of the Sea is often pictured. But we remained for the most part an undifferentiated cluster, a passel of kids who swarmed at family gatherings. Růžena would beam, her apple cheeks crinkling invitingly, but few of the children grasped how to get past her charisma, past the "idea" of great-grandmother, and experience the up-close infusion of love we knew awaited us.

It wasn't till I was 15 or so that I had my first audience with Růžena. She was living in Queens with her daughter Mollie at the time, and mother and I stopped by for a visit. After refreshments were offered, Růžena invited us into her bedroom to show me samples of needlework she'd done as a girl. In those days, all girls were required to excel at crocheting, she explained in her quavery, sing-songey voice as she fingered her perfect handiwork. Now, surveying this scene, it was my mother's turn to beam.

I knew that if I were to travel to Růžena's hometown, I would have to learn her language, and so I began my Czech studies one year ago. It was my sixth foreign language and, like the others, it has pointed up the superiorities and shortcomings of English. With Czech, for some reason, I had the sense, much more acutely than with previous linguistic undertakings, that all languages are exactly the same. Each is familiar to me because it is human, after all, expressing the same gamut of human emotions, humor, irony, vexation, and delight no matter what the tongue.

That said, it never fails to amaze me the sheer diversity of words and grammars and morphologies—the Babel of it all! Czech, for instance, manages its nouns with hair-splitting precision, dividing them into four genders and seven cases, and a Czech speaker is on intimate terms with the life of a noun. An English speaker functions with an excess of freedom, on the other hand—his nouns, uninflected, serve many purposes, even transmute into adjectives and verbs with no exertion on his part.

Each language offers a different physical experience as well. In contrast with the roundness of Portuguese, English feels flat and flaccid, puny in the mouth. America is a nation of mumblers, our lips barely moving.

Czech, however, demands vigorous articulation, the consequence of frequent collision of consonants. I love all the "z" words—a common letter in the language—because they seem to deliver a jolt of electricity: *zitra, zima, zmrzlina, zlý.*

Most of Růžena's great-grandchildren are prosperous burghers now, as she herself had become, and they have reproduced themselves, carrying her DNA into an American future. There's a rogue gene in me that instead looks backward to the land of castles, longing for the idea of her, the source of her, seeking to discover an unknown part of myself.

From the class journal.

HOW TO ROPE A CALF

Jenna Buffaloe

MY FRIEND DANI GREW UP on a ranch in Sprague, Washington, 36 miles west of Spokane. Now Dani is an engineer at Microsoft in Seattle, but her family still works the ranch. Each year in the spring, 30 or so of her 30-something Seattle friends travel over the Cascades to help with the yearly roundup, where the new calves are branded, inoculated, and castrated. Each year I meant to go, but work and life always intervened.

This year was different. I was unemployed. I'd quit my well-paying, do-gooding, sexy job, what everyone told me was one of the best jobs in Seattle, because my boss was a petty tyrant, and because I was craving something, something I still couldn't put my finger on, some internal unfolding and reorganizing that could only be done in a jobless space.

When I stopped working it had been summer. I had some money, but tried not to spend it, and was happy to do free things, like swim with friends in Lake Washington, jump off the high dive, pick blackberries and make jam. But then fall set in, and the sun sank earlier each day and reappeared later each morning. It was dark as midnight from four in the afternoon until nine the next morning. It rained for 30 days straight. My bank account balance dwindled with the sunlight, because now this season of unemployment had gone on longer than I had anticipated. I stopped calling friends to go out, because going out cost money. I sold my car to pay another month's mortgage. When I didn't get a job I'd applied for, I heard that I, an overachieving Harvard grad, had developed a reputation for being flighty, and unable to hold down a job. My confidence was shot, my internal self still tangled.

But then the days grew longer, and were occasionally clear, and I could feel a shift coming. And even though nothing had really changed, I felt my spirits lifting. So this year, when Dani called to invite me to the roundup, I said yes.

My ex-boyfriend Caleb, who had only recently forgiven me for falling in love with someone else and leaving him three years before, was driving east to Montana to fish the Clark Fork for a week, and offered to drop me off at Dani's ranch. He picked me up at my Seattle apartment early on a foggy morning, bearing cinnamon rolls and orange juice and a thermos of coffee.

As we headed out of town toward Snoqualamie Pass, we talked about his work and my lack of, our families and his becoming an uncle, our new theories on relationships and why ours didn't work out. We drove in silence for a while, then talked about bigger things, spiritual things like Planet Earth and the Milky Way, and why whales evolved from the land back into the sea, and if humans might do the same. Listening to him I remembered why I fell for him in the first place. I forgot our fragile friendship and turned around to see if we could make some room in the back to lie down. But it was packed to the roof with two large coolers, a tent and a sleeping bag, a pair of waders, and a rubber inner-tube. I did not kiss him when we stopped for gas.

East of the mountains, it was sunny and windy. We arrived at the roundup midmorning, surrounded by herds of people and cows and vast stretches of open land. Dani was roasting hot dogs outside a corral, wearing an apron and a red bandanna around her short brown hair. Caleb greeted her—they are friends from high school—then waved goodbye to us and moved on to the fish in Montana.

The cattle had already been brought down from the pasture. I had a camera, but what I really needed was a recorder, for the mooing was awesome and deafening. Dani's cousins were in the ring on horseback, chasing the cattle from behind and then opening and closing gates to separate the calves from the cows and steers. The calves were several months old, and already two and three hundred pounds. The entire herd looked sincere and distressed, heads lowered as they were separated from their kin. I knew they were stressed because of all the diarrhea, the universal sign of stress.

I ate a hot dog with relish and mustard. Someone handed me a beer.

A group of rough-looking men in chaps gathered at one end of the ring. I asked Dani who they were. "Professional ropers," she said. "From north of Spokane. They're part of a religious group that practices polygamy." She thought so anyway. She wasn't sure if they really did.

It took a while to separate out the calves. Once they were corralled, and the adult cows and steers were off in another fenced-in pasture, the real work began. The city folk were expected to finish their hot dogs and beers, and gather in the ring. I decided I would hang back for a minute and see what happened.

A dozen professional ropers got on their horses and lined up in the ring. The first one in line rode into the smaller corral of calves and swung his lasso above his head. He threw the rope and hit a calf in the leg. Just as he hit it, the calf lifted his leg, and the cowboy tugged on the rope, catching the calf by the hoof. The crowd threw up a yell. The cowboy spurred his horse out of the ring, ducking as he went, for the bar over the gate was low enough to take him off his horse. The calf was fighting on three legs, but soon the momentum was too much for him, and he was thrown off balance onto his back. Now the city folk in the ring, five or so for each calf, most of whom had done this many years in a row, rushed the calf and held it down while it was snipped, clipped, burned, and inoculated. The calf was fighting and mooing and pooing.

The cowboys on their horses continued to ride one by one into the corral. They didn't always come out with a calf. When one missed a throw, he'd ride out of the corral back into the ring with an empty rope behind him, recoil the rope, and get back in line. The good ropers got a calf most times they rode into the ring. A few of the younger cowboys roped only a handful throughout the day.

The whole thing was unnervingly violent. I was not sure I wanted to be a part of it, though I was no novice to slaughter. When I was 15 I worked as a junior counselor at Jameson Ranch, the summer camp in the Sierra foothills where I had been a camper. Junior counselors were responsible for the ranch chores, which included shooting a cow each Tuesday, stringing it up, and packing the meat. I felt there was nothing wrong with this practice—these cows had wonderful lives until the moment we sent them home to their creator—but I had no taste for meat, not even chicken, for 13 years. Then one day, a couple years ago, an overwhelming urge to eat bacon seized me, and so I ate some. Now I eat bacon every chance I get, and other meat occasionally.

But this was different than the peaceful slaughter—one bullet to the head—that I was used to. These calves were fighting, outraged and afraid. Surprisingly, they fought harder against the branding than the testicle slicing. Watching from the sidelines, I felt their pain. I wanted to leave. It was windy and I was sleepy, and I wanted to set up my tent, crawl in it and take a nap. But the hypocrisy of that plan was too obvious: as long as I eat meat and wear leather, I had no business taking a nap and leaving this work to others. Also, I had a funny feeling. I felt I was being called to do something.

And so, with some reluctance, I pulled off my sweatshirt, pulled on a pair of leather gloves, and stepped into the ring.

The first calf I approached hesitantly, and immediately learned my lesson. A hoof went into my thigh, leaving a bruise the size of an orange. There was blood on my arm and my jeans, but I didn't know where it came from, or if it was mine or the calf's. After that first calf I understood that there was no doing this halfway. You were either in completely, all your weight upon the calf, all your bicep strength holding back a leg, or you were bound to get kicked, hard. I was bloody and filthy and wounded, but completely committed to this task.

Dani's boyfriend was in charge of inoculating. This was appropriate, for in real life he's a phlebotomist. Dani's cousin carried big scissors, and she was clipping calf ears. Another man came over with a hot branding iron and sank it into the animal's flesh, sending smoke into the air and eliciting fresh screams from the calf.

Then an older cowboy strode over. He had laughing blue eyes and a very sharp knife. He kneeled on one knee and sliced open the furry bottom of the scrotum. Then he put the knife handle between his teeth and with his thick tanned fingers squeezed out (like a hen laying an egg) two white, fatty, bloody testicles.

When we didn't need his services we yelled out "heifer!" I thanked God each time a calf we tackled turned out to be a heifer, and thanked God that I, myself, am a heifer. The man with the knife really wanted to make me his apprentice, but I declined. I had karma to consider, and made it a policy not to do things I would have to explain to my mythical husband someday.

Hours later, with about half of the calves done and a new crop of city folks doing the wrestling, I approached a cowboy—older than the rest—in line on his horse. I'd had my eye on this cowboy and his horse. They were a team, these two. They came out with a calf each time they went into the ring, and there was no tension between them the way there was with other cowboys who'd picked horses maybe a little too wild. Neither this cowboy nor this horse had anything to prove. I learned later that this cowboy was the one who taught all the cowboys in Spokane County how to rope.

Now I asked him if I could borrow his rope. "Sure," he said, and leaned down to hand it to me.

When I was a camper at Jameson Ranch, I used to practice roping. Every afternoon I stood in front of a fence post, swinging the lasso above my head and throwing it in the direction of the post. I got better with practice, and twice a summer old Mr. Jameson would take us into a mess of calves to try roping their necks. I caught the fence post many times, and by my fifth summer at Jameson Ranch I could catch the neck of a calf too. At some point I began practicing roping not just at camp, but at home during the year as well. It was a familiar sight to see me in our front yard—two blocks from the beach and many miles from any cows—with my lasso, aiming at our fence post.

The rope I had practiced with was soft, like a mountaineering rope. This cowboy's rope was stiff, a real lariat. I had practiced roping from above, catching a fence post in preparation for roping a calf's neck. This was roping from below, to catch a leg.

I stepped out of the ring, and called over Dani's dark handsome friend, Max. I asked him to stand 20 feet away from me and dance like a calf. He did. I swung the lariat above my head, threw it, caught his ankle, and pulled the rope to tighten the knot. This surprised Max, who seemed grateful that I did not then pull him onto his back and slice off his testicles.

Never mind that I had never roped from a horse before. Never mind that the last time I rode a horse was ten years before, and that I fell off at breakneck speed and landed in the emergency room.

From my perch on a fence post I asked the cowboy whose rope I'd borrowed, "Can I borrow your horse?"

"Sure," he said. I hadn't expected him to say yes. "But the stirrups are going to be too long for you," he said as he swung his long leg over and hopped down to the ground. He was a tall drink of water, as we say in Sprague, Washington. I proposed we shorten them, but he said they didn't shorten.

I stepped my foot in the stirrup and swung my leg over. I found my seat and my balance, and reached down to acquaint myself with the horse with a rough pat on his horse's neck. I held the coiled rope in my left hand, and the stiff circle of lariat in my right. Legs dangling like I was riding bareback, I rode into the corral of calves. I swung the rope around my head and threw it. It landed in a tangled mess on the ground. The calves looked at me with large, barely blinking eyes. They didn't bother to move or moo, and wondered, I'm sure, what I thought I was doing there. As I rode out, my rope dragged on the ground, and I nearly roped the hoof of my borrowed horse. But I was exhilarated that I had tried and didn't need to go to the emergency room.

"Nice try," said the cowboy. He smiled at me, and I gave him back his horse.

Ten minutes later we were there again, I on the fence and he in line. "Hey," I said. "Can I borrow your horse again?" Again, he said yes.

I got back on the horse. Sitting in the saddle, I asked the cowboy, "What do I do once I catch the calf's leg?"

He shook his head. "You don't need to worry about it," he said, "because you're not going to catch one." There was nothing belittling in his tone, it was just a realistic assessment of the situation from someone who had seen a lot.

Throughout the winter, I prayed often, "Thy will, not mine." I'd become suspicious of my own willfulness and determination, sensing I didn't have the wisdom to handle these traits. I tried letting things happen instead.

But when this cowboy told me I would not succeed, something deep, long dormant, stirred. A familiar rush of determination overwhelmed me, and I did not deny it. I understood that I could trust myself now, to know when to step into the ring and when to hang back. I had hung back long enough. It was time to step back in.

"Oh yeah?" I thought, when he told me this. I felt then that I could do anything, and rode into the corral knowing I would be coming out with a calf.

This time, I got right on top of the cluster of calves. I swung the lasso above my head. As it left my hand, I knew that it was a perfect throw. And as it left my hand, time slowed down and everything went quiet. The rope landed on the back of a calf and began to slide down its leg. The calf reacted to the rope by lifting its leg. As the loop in the rope passed its hoof, I gave a sharp tug. I felt the knot slide down the rope. I felt the calf's hoof in my knot. And then I felt him yank back—like the tug of a fish caught on a line.

I did not know how strong he would be. I had mistakenly imagined riding out of the ring, rope in one hand, dragging the calf behind me. But the instant he began to fight, the rope was ripping out of my bare hands. I needed leverage, which I figured just then was what the horn of the saddle must be for. Like I'd done it all my life, I wrapped the rope twice around the horn.

Noise and time came back, and everyone was yelling and the calf was fighting like crazy. "Go! Go!" yelled my cowboy coach. I spurred the horse out of the ring, ducking as we went through the gate. I was pulling three hundred pounds of crazed calf behind me, and it was a challenge to stay in the saddle. I would have felt better with my feet in stirrups. We fought our way into the middle of the corral. The calf was flipped off its feet and tackled by the crew. "Now let go of the rope!" yelled the cowboy. I did.

Thank God it was a heifer.

WE GATHERED THAT NIGHT at the tavern in Sprague. As I walked into the bar, I saw my cowboy friends sitting at a table drinking pitchers of

Bud. I started to walk up to them but stopped when I heard they were talking about me. "Goddamn," said one. "She did that without stirrups."

Another shook his head. "She could've done it without a bridle," he said.

The first cowboy saw me standing there and stood up. "Hey you!" he said. "When you gonna give me a lesson?"

The cowboys and city folk mingled together, dancing and singing karaoke. I wanted to dance, but my success had made me self-conscious. I was aware of people looking at me, wondering what else I could do. One friend of a cowboy, a correctional officer at the State Pen in Spokane, had wondered if I might marry him that afternoon, and I didn't want to encourage him. So I hung back on a stool, swaying and moving but sticking to the seat.

But finally I couldn't take it anymore. For the second time that day, I pulled off my sweatshirt. Dancing this time, I must have looked like I was about to begin a striptease. But I didn't care. Finally, I didn't care who was looking at me. I would hold nothing back. For I was done pretending I am not this alive and this determined. I was done pretending I don't shake my butt like this. I was done pretending I don't know how to hop on a horse, ride into the ring, and rope a calf.

HEALING WORDS

AFTER PARIS

Elizabeth A. Montgomery

BEFORE TWO WHITE-COATED MEN in rubber-soled shoes had probed my breast with needles, before I had vomited from the combined effects of anesthesia and the word "malignant," before I rested in high-backed vinyl chairs with red and blue liquids flowing through me, before I lost my hair and my breast, before I swam in restless dreams of morphine, I was in Paris.

My mother was nearly 70. She traveled with other widows, bridge partners, at least three times a year. Travel and her friends had buoyed her life for the five years since my father's death. One day, on the phone—we live a continent apart—we talked about the restoration of Monet's gardens, in Giverny, and I said we should see the gardens together.

This wistful thought was turned by my mother into a proposal for a family trip. My husband and I and my brother and his wife would accompany her to Paris. Without our children. This gift, I thought, must be her way of saying "Who knows how many more trips I have in me? Come with me, share in my life's pleasures while they last." Fugitive pleasures would, in fact, become this journey's enduring theme.

And so, at the end of May 1994, I awoke in a Paris hotel. Freshly washed streets steamed in the early morning sunlight. The sun rose into a deep blue sky, periodically obscured by rapidly moving masses of white and gray clouds. Late spring was turning into early summer; the leaves of the trees were still a fresh green. On that first morning, in a nearby park, I discovered a group of four- and five-year-olds watching, open-mouthed, as Punch and Judy batted at one another, stage curtains flailing with each blow.

True to plan, my mother, sister-in-law, and I took a day trip to Giverny. After leaving the highway our enormous tour bus lumbered along like an elephant in a line with six or seven others through the narrow village streets that led to Monet's house. To my surprise, not even crowds moving through the narrow corridors of the house or slowing my passage through the allées of the gardens dampened my pleasure in this place. People seemed to hush under the influence of the gardens' saturated color—at this season predominantly reds and yellows, poppies and nasturtium. Quiet ruled in the light and shadow of the wooded walks near the lily-covered pond crossed by the Pont Japonais.

On other days, we wandered through Paris, satisfying our different interests, as couples, as threesomes, or as blissfully unencumbered single adults. We met in my mother's suite each evening for drinks and we would all go to dinner together. One night, we emerged from the Métro into an arcade of flowers, mostly climbing roses, tagged with names like Duchesse de Pompadour or Sombreuil, growing on arched trellises down the median of a boulevard. Seeking a restaurant well known to natives but not to tourists, we had taken the wrong Métro line and had blocks and blocks to walk. It was fine, though, getting lost in this residential neighborhood, in a way that getting lost in large cities rarely is. We became lightheaded, walking hungrily through air and light filtered by the scent and color of rose petals.

Finally, a line of Parisian families waiting impatiently for its doors to open drew us to the restaurant's anonymous corner facade. The insider's strategy, we were told, requires joining the queue before the 7:00 p.m. opening. We were swept in at 20 minutes after seven, famished from our walk. Our waitress spun from table to table. With a menu limited to steak, frites, red wine, and dessert, ordering was blissfully efficient. Just how bloody did we want our steaks to be, and which of the five red wines did we prefer?

We savored our tender steaks and large plates of thin frites, drank from bottles of the best Bordeaux, and chose desserts from a tray that must have measured a meter across. We watched, with pleasure, Parisian parents tutoring their children in restaurant etiquette. We were outsiders who, after a wrong turn, had found their way into a palace of simple but sublime comfort. We were four parents and a grandparent who at this very moment missed their young boys both very much and not at all.

I went alone to the Louvre, back to the museum's many rooms of antiquities, my first visit since my college days, two decades before. Then, and now, I photographed Roman and Greek and Egyptian carved stone in black and white. I wanted to capture the mystery and the muscles, rippling skin carved from cold stone, exotic features frozen in time, many centuries ago.

Standing close to Aphrodite's outstretched arm, I focused the camera lens on her long slender fingers, curled lightly around a perfectly round ball. My photograph captures her rounded shoulders, a serene classical profile with a high brow flowing from flat, carved curls held down with marble ribbons, her long neck, and her perfect right breast. She is holding the golden apple of Discordia, awarded to her by Paris, who has judged her most beautiful of goddesses. She has wrested the apple away from Hera and Athena by offering to Paris the love of Helen, the most beautiful of mortal women. Aphrodite will soon launch the Trojan War by luring Helen from her husband. The sculptor has captured her moment of triumph without foreshadowing the bloodshed to come.

Our hotel, close to the fashionable shopping avenues of the Right Bank, but protected from their traffic by a maze of narrow streets, offered rooms of many different shapes and sizes. The room where my husband and I slept had ballroom-high ceilings with elaborate crown moldings. The scale of the room dwarfed the double bed, but the carved wood armoire, perhaps ten feet high and eight feet wide, fit perfectly. Three shuttered floor-to-ceiling windows with small balconies ran the length of the room. They opened to and looked out upon a narrow street of apartments and a school, where families dropped off children in the morning, and out of which children spilled in the afternoon. The furnishings were a little worn, but the bathroom had been updated to the standards of Casa Vogue. It contained a lovely soaking tub, short but deep, well stocked with fragrant bath salts.

Eight years later, I can clearly see that room. On the day of our departure, while we were packing, I found a spot of blood on a crease of the cool, starchy linen case of the feather pillow that I had drawn close the night before. I stood in the middle of that outsize, century-old room, and I opened my bra. There was just a little discoloration. I went into the bathroom, closed the door behind me, and ran cool water through the pillowcase and bra until it ran clear into the sleek French porcelain sink.

The radiologist who had reviewed my mammogram and sonogram six months before, when the lump was first found, had sent me home cleared of danger. He had made a mistake. When I left Paris I couldn't know that, but I did know that a bloody discharge from my nipple was a sign that something was very wrong. I kept my fear from my husband. I said nothing to my mother, my brother, or my sister-in-law. A week later, a man I barely knew drew back the curtains of my outpatient surgery cubicle to tell me that he didn't need to wait for the pathology report: he had bad news.

I had smelled lush old French roses in the heat and dampness of an early summer night on the streets of Paris. I had waited in a mirrored hotel lobby with an old open-grillwork lift, immersed in a language I had learned from literature. I had slept wrapped in cool linen sheets warmed with a soft down duvet. I had wakened to the history written on the high ceilings of my room. Every morning for a week I had ordered coffee and almond croissants at a pâtisserie and shopped the designer windows on the Avenue Montaigne. I had visited the Arc de Triomphe at sunrise, alone, and listened to the city roar itself awake.

Now I lay on a succession of hard padded examination tables in cold rooms with linoleum floors, gazed at charts depicting the stages of cancer, looked up at fluorescent lights hanging from asbestos tiles. I waited in green corridors on folding chairs, or on worn upholstery in waiting rooms with faded travel posters. I stripped, waist up, again and again until I became adept at securing the tangled ties of faded cotton hospital gowns. My blood was drawn and my veins were tapped and filled with toxic, life-saving chemicals. I listened to the stories of other cancer patients, to my own statistics, and to the Greek and Latin of medical terminology. My family and I talked of treatments, and prognoses.

For months, I kept the picture of my Aphrodite in the Louvre on my bedroom mirror, and sometimes looked at my reflection, naked from the waist up, beside it. The photograph reminded me of the six additional months of innocence granted to me by a misread mammogram. What drew me to her? Why did I focus my camera on her right breast, the one I would lose three months later? Aphrodite's apple, symbol of mortal folly and destruction, is a small ball not much larger than the five centimeters of my tumor, held away from her body, at arm's length. Aphrodite has turned away from it. She is very strong, very beautiful and youthful. She is serene, and she is immortal.

This essay is dedicated to the former and surviving members of the Post–Bone Marrow Transplant Support Group.

FLOWERS AS TEACHERS

Bonnie Epstein

I CLIP A FEW DOZEN ROSES from the prolific bushes in my yard, wrap them in dripping paper towels tucked into tin foil, and place them on the back seat of my Honda. I drive to Dr. O's office in a perfumed car.

The bells tinkle as I open the office door. Dr. O looks up. Her face merges surprise and glee. "For me? From your garden?" She moves toward the bouquet with outstretched arms as if reaching for an infant.

"Yes."

"So many. And smell wonderful." Her nose bobs from one to the next. "You save some for yourself?"

"I have 20 bushes. Too many for myself." I smile as I hear my broken sentences. I'm starting to talk like her.

"Beautiful, beautiful. Look, many colors. Yellow. Pink. Red, dark red." She coos as she displays them to the others in the room. Dr. O chooses a vase with care from her collection on the bookcase and leaves for the bathroom, her source of water.

In her absence my attention opens to the sounds in the room, songs of friendliness sung by the choir of patients filling most of the chairs. The air feels welcoming. My mind relaxes into silence.

I take one of the two unoccupied seats. "The roses, they're a lot of work, huh?" the woman on my left inquires.

"Oh, yes. I inherited them when I bought the house. Little did I know what I let myself in for." I hold out my arm to exhibit my battle wounds. "My arm and the thorns tangle, arm loses. But the roses are worth it. They're beautiful and bring lots of pleasure."

Dr. O reappears with the flowers arranged in a glorious display. She places the vase on the corner of her desk, steps back a few paces, looks, moves forward, adjusts a couple of stems, steps back again and nods.

"More balance now?" She glances in my direction.

"They look beautiful. Like from a florist's. Never have my roses been given such attention."

"Flowers are my friends." She returns to her chair, her face a smile, and addresses the male patient at her desk. "So, how you bowels?"

Her words, "flowers are my friends," replay in my mind like a song sung in a deep canyon. My heart dances. This is what I want to learn, to live in that kind of sentence. I close my eyes and take a few quiet breaths to etch that sentence into my cells. I inhale the richness she brings to my life.

SEVERAL WEEKS PASS before I am driven by my ovary-deprived hormones to call for another appointment. My meltdowns occur when my glasses aren't where I swear I put them; when everything I touch lands on the floor; when the pages of the newspaper stick together; when the jar cap won't budge no matter how many times I whack it with the knife handle. These frustrations, though accompanied by tears, do not plunge me into a pool of worthlessness. I ask myself only once or twice what I'm doing wrong. Dr. O's words—"Not doing wrong. Just life"—provide the answer. I interpret my acceptance of this nonjudgmental view as psychological growth, and credit to it Dr. O's unrelenting pummelings. I strut around a bit peacockish about the new me.

But during the second or two that my denial system abandons its post, I acknowledge that the occasional chocolate chip cookie and the more occasional mocha ice cream that have snuck themselves into my diet may have something to do with my current imbalance.

I arrive at Dr. O's bearing flowers and urine. She nods at me as I enter and continues with the man seated by her desk. She is busy this morning; both tables are occupied and a man and woman are waiting.

I put my purse, paper bag, book, and flowers on a chair, choose a vase from her collection, and head to the bathroom to fill it.

"Where you going?" she barks at me as I open the door.

"For water." I hold the vase toward her.

"I do. Don't worry."

"I'm not worried. You're busy so I'll do it. You can arrange them when you're finished." I nod towards the patient at her desk. "It's okay for me to help. You help everyone. Now it's my turn to help you. And this is a very tiny help."

She says nothing. Just stares at me, one eyebrow raised above the rim of her glasses. Then turns her attention back to the curly-haired man who's telling her about his painful knees.

I don't know this stare. Mad? Glad? Questioning? I hope I haven't insulted her. These worries tumble around in my brain while water fills the vase. I return, tiptoeing, plunk the freesias into their new home, and set them on the table next to me to avoid any further disruption. As their fragrance sweetens the air I notice I am not berating myself for causing a ruckus. It's simple. The freesias needed water and I gave it to them. If Dr. O's upset, it's her problem. I'm. . .

"Why you put flowers by you? You bring for me and keep for you?"

I collapse with laughter. "Has anyone ever told you how impossible you are?" I spit out as I hurtle to her desk with the unarranged flowers. "I was trying not to interrupt. Not be a pest. I can't win, can I?" I wave the vase over her desk and with my eyes ask her where to place it. She points to the right edge.

"What you trying win?" She looks like an alley cat who has cornered her prey.

"I just want to do something right once in my life. To win that. Not too much to ask, is it?" I stumble back to my seat.

"C'mon! What right? Right for who? You right for you, good intention, then okay." Her voice rings out as her head falls back and thrusts her chin into the air. All eyes peer at me, the class troublemaker. I half expect her to send me to the principal's office.

"Don't worry. Be happy. Not thinking if right or not. Just do. With heart. Put mind on flowers, not on right." She raps me on the top of my head with her knuckles as she pushes her bewildered, limping patient toward the back room.

I rub the spot she knuckled as I fill with amazement. Everything is a teaching for her. A "wake up to your thinking" lesson. I'm boggled at how the simple act of getting water in a vase for flowers can be fodder for growth. True, I was not present with the act. I was worrying about her look, about interrupting, about being a pest. Melodramas from my childhood performed on my mental stage 55 years later. Appalling. Still reading faces because Mother's face told the truth when her words lied. I am still carrying those fears. . . of being blamed, wrong, disliked. Dr. O hears my brain's whirling words.

"Still thinking," she scolds and raps me again on her return trip.

"I better move before I end up with a hole in my head," I squawk and pat the stinging spot. I catch her thought before she can speak it. "Yeah, yeah, I know. A hole in my head would be good for letting the thoughts fall out."

Freesias, laughter, and the clapping of her two strong hands fill the air.

Excerpted from a memoir entitled *Healing Needles*. The writer is an eleven-year survivor of uterine and ovarian cancer. She had a hysterectomy and then chose acupuncture as her follow-up treatment. *Healing Needles* is the story of the physical, psychological, and spiritual transformation that resulted from the writer's post-cancer acupuncture treatments and the relationship between doctor and patient.

DAYS OF LEAD

Kara Jane Rollins

THE TIMES ALONE IN THE HOSPITAL are the worst, the times when the real mothers are settling down for the night, knowing their babies are safe in the nursery and will be going home with them. I have difficulty sleeping and stand by the window, smoking and carrying my great hollow body around with me, a swollen pod that has lost its contents. My stomach protrudes and people think I haven't had the baby yet, this child who is going home with other parents. Someone down in the patient lobby yesterday asked me when I was due and my face burned. This is my first baby, and I don't realize that this bloated stomach will eventually go away and my breasts will return to normal size. I feel as if this physical state will continue forever. I escape as quickly as possible from all questioners, not wanting to talk, but not knowing how to get away, as if explaining to the world is my punishment. Were I freer, I would lumber down the hallway, like the lopsided alien thing that I am, knocking over carts and bruising the walls, screaming that this childbirth has pushed me past the boundaries of sanity. But I am careful to observe my mood and remain stable, perhaps even hopeful about the future.

The hospital staff has been protecting me from contact with other new mothers by putting me on a different floor. But last night a fellow patient drifted into my room, her black curly hair ruffled, her eyes burning, her cheeks flecked with color. I thought of Ophelia's madness when I looked at her. This patient had obviously escaped her room and flapped her way upstairs, a wounded mother bird, wild and distracted. She asked me the inevitable questions about the baby's sex, weight, father. I made up lies, mumbling, ashamed of who I am and what I am doing. She told me that she had two baby girls that morning and they both died. Her face did not change when she said it and I could not speak. A nurse came in and gently encouraged her away, giving me a look of apology. I was supposed to be spared this kind of connection.

Tom brings me flowers and candy as if I have had an appendectomy and not his child. He brings his roommate Ron to cheer me. I can tell they are both uncomfortable, but trying to make this as easy as possible. We talk in pleasantries and laugh about the gritty granules the nurses give me in a paper cup each morning because I am constipated. The ghost of pain hovers in the room and we are both aware of it, but keep our silence. I am haunted by images. The night she was born Tom waited in the family lounge, smoking a whole pack of Marlboros. They wheeled me back to the room, an empty body with a sunken stomach, but alive, excited, not sure where to put those unplanned feelings. They ushered him in, the infamous father of this baby. When we were alone, he put his face on my legs and sobbed, great sobs that shook us both. He told me he was worried that something would happen to me during those long hours behind closed doors, but I knew that he cried for her, for us, and for himself. Tomorrow a married couple will take her home, this little one I try not to think about. I will go to see her in the morning. Someone told me that seeing her again would be the emotionally healthy thing to do. They say it will make it real and give me some closure. I light another cigarette and stare out at the night.

THANKFUL TO THE MARROW

Terri Hinte

AT ANY GIVEN MOMENT, all my life, I've been blessed with whatever I needed—money, love, an unexpected belly laugh—to get through the day and the dark night. Very often my cup has overflowed and filled the empty vessels of those around me. I have an abiding faith that it will always be thus.

So it was surprising to me how quickly my sturdy faith crumpled upon hearing the news, five autumns ago, that my baby brother John was suddenly dying of cancer.

It was, quite simply, impossible. Dad had just died two years before; my maternal grandfather (and sole surviving grandparent) followed a year later. Death had been to our door, thank you very much! I *did not* want to relinquish this beautiful boy.

John had visited me in Berkeley that summer. He was about to turn 23, and with his newly minted degree in painting was looking forward to getting a job. He had an in at Marvel Comics, where during two summer internships he'd forged close ties with several editors.

He was looking a bit ascetic, I thought. Our middle brother Jim, a tall, slim tennis player, had always said that John, with his husky build and dancer's grace, could excel at football. Right now he resembled a Romantic poet.

Several times during our visit, he complained to me about back pain. He was seeing a chiropractor in New York, and though X-rays didn't reveal much of anything he'd signed up for a series of treatments. We discussed yoga and other alternative approaches to back problems.

That was June. In September he was entering the hospital for what turned out to be a month's stay. He endured endless tests, which proved inconclusive. His case was stumping specialists at Columbia and Sloan-Kettering. It was one for the books, they said. Weeks passed as the doctors debated. Daily, the patient deteriorated. It appeared to be cancer, and was already in his spine; his upper vertebrae were disintegrating. But a precise diagnosis still eluded those paid to know.

By the time I saw him again, in October, he was frail as a bird in his hospital bed and desperately frightened. X-rays and tissue samples continued to make the rounds as John slipped away from us.

Tormented by this glacial pace, my mother made an emotional "mother-to-mother" appeal to the hospital president to kindly get the doctors in gear before the patient expired. *"Somebody do something!"* was the gist of it. The very next day, plans were set in motion to transfer John to a larger county hospital with more extensive cancer-treatment facilities.

It was there he met Dr. A., who took charge of his case. After studying John's thick file, Dr. A. was as perplexed as the doctors before him. He never did determine the primary site of the cancer. But, hazarding a guess and following his instincts, he settled on a name for the illness: B-cell lymphoma.

B-cells. What were *they*? *Where* were they? The doctor never explained. But John's had run amok, and were snuffing out his life. Untreated, they would kill him in a few short months.

When Dr. A. proposed a bone-marrow transplant as our only hope, I knew instantly that I would be the donor. Despite our age difference—I was nearly 17 when John arrived during our family's exile in Lynchburg, Virginia—I'd always felt that he and I shared an out-of-the-ordinary bond. For starters, I was tapped as his one and only godparent, since Jim and I had already depleted the small stock of aunts and uncles who were suitable candidates. Though at that time my Catholicism was well on its way to lapsing, I was still in awe of the prospect of gaining a godchild, of the ritual of washing away a newborn's sins—of standing in, even, for God as the infant's spiritual guardian. Should something befall the parents—our parents—I would also bear responsibility for his material welfare.

What I learned, as John's berserk B-cells rampaged, was that a sibling or parent had just a one-in-four chance of providing a bone-marrow match. Yet our pool of one mother, one brother, and one sister yielded the necessary genetic twin—me.

Three long months passed. John suffered through a punishing series of chemotherapy treatments. The minutes, to use Edna O'Brien's phrase, were rugged. Finally, in February, I found myself in an upstate New York hospital bed down the hall from the ailing John. The bone-marrow ward had to protect its residents from the possibly lethal effects of the commonest microbes, and so visitors wore white surgical masks. Everyone washed hands frequently. Flowers were not permitted.

For a week before my arrival, John's body was bombarded by a blitzkrieg of radiation and chemotherapy that aimed to shut down what was left of his failed immune system. Not one white blood cell would survive.

My body was the chalice containing the elixir that could restore John's life. A pint was "harvested" from my pelvic bones with outsize sucking needles and transfused into his virtual corpse. (My name, Teresa, comes from the Greek, "bearer of harvest.") But it was no sure thing. His suitemate Anthony, whose own family had stood vigil as two of their sons underwent this slow-motion ordeal, didn't make it. The preparatory chemo had destroyed Anthony's liver. His brother's perfectly-matching marrow was poured into the fallow ground of Anthony's body.

John did make it. My white blood cells transubstantiated into his. His battered body withstood the rigors of reentry into life, into the perpetual rallying against enemies seen and unseen. With time, his fears of annihilation have subsided somewhat. Though his hair seems reluctant to grow back, John has returned to his artist's notebook. And, much to our amazement, he's taken up golf with a vengeance.

THE HEART OF THE MATTER

Kathleen Faraday & Joan Stevenson

KATHLEEN WRITES: I woke with a throbbing headache early on Sunday morning. My daughter Emily and I were staying at a charming Tahoe B&B. We'd had a wonderful day of skiing and were all ready for another. I tiptoed to the bathroom and took two Excedrin. It was still two hours before time to get up—my head would stop pounding by then. Suddenly my headache progressed into vomiting. Now what? Surely it wasn't my prime rib and cosmopolitan (only one!) the night before. Altitude had never been a problem. I lay back carefully, knowing it would subside.

Finally we were forced to accept that I was in no shape to ski. I felt sabotaged by my own body. Emily loaded up the car and we headed for home. It took six hours in a snowstorm to creep down the mountain with chains and many stops for me to hang my head out the window. I couldn't even keep water down. As we finally crossed the Benicia Bridge, I mumbled, "I just can't wait to crawl into my own bed."

"Oh, no, Mom," Emily commanded, "I'm not taking you home— we are going straight to John Muir." I protested weakly, but realized that I was not improving.

Things moved very quickly at John Muir Hospital, and as the nurse put on the blood pressure cuff, I remembered my doctor saying a few months earlier that we needed to watch my blood pressure because it seemed to be creeping up. I took little notice other than the vague memory of that comment. I was too healthy. I asked the nurse, "Is my blood pressure high?"

"It is ridiculously high," she snapped, and before I knew it I was whisked off in a wheelchair and onto a bed, hooked up to God knows what, and trying desperately not to throw up in the middle of the CAT scan. No luck!

My oldest daughter phoned and I assured her, "Oh, honey, don't worry, I am fine." Next thing I knew, she and her husband casually walked into the ER, passing off lightly the fact that they had just canceled their first anniversary dinner. That got my attention. I was on the precipice of a stroke.

High blood pressure is the silent killer and mine was like a powder keg. But why me? I eat right, exercise religiously, what more could I do? "Nothing" was my doctor's response. "It is genetic." My dad had emergency bypass surgery, but he smoked and his idea of exercise was a round of golf. It is a difficult concept for me to grasp, but I feel blessed, because mine surfaced with a vengeance. Check out the statistics! Fifty percent of women over 55 have high blood pressure! I'm not unique, just lucky, because mine is treated—is yours?

JOAN WRITES: Finding myself in the emergency room at John Muir Hospital was like an out-of-body experience. It was as if I was standing in the corner of the sterile cubicle observing the cardiologist telling a stranger she had just failed the stress test and that she would not be leaving the hospital. Not me, I thought. It just could not be.

I prided myself on maintaining a healthy lifestyle. I was a regular on the trail in the morning, running for years and walking when I could no longer keep up the pace of my companions 20 years younger. I was careful what I ate and in recent years leaned more toward the vegetarian diet. I had given up smoking 30 years before. My cholesterol level was slightly elevated but not of real concern. I enjoyed a busy lifestyle so I didn't really think of it as stress.

The symptom that sent me to the cardiologist was a recurring pain in my jaw. I experienced it every morning for a week at the same slight rise on the trail around the reservoir. It came swiftly and left me a bit breathless. It would dissipate just as quickly and I would feel fine. Then it came one night and was so severe that I slept with my cheek on a heating pad. That evening the pain radiated down my left arm. Because it started in my jaw, I determined it was a temporomandibular joint problem. I called the dentist to ask what treatment he would recommend. There was a long pause before he replied, "Joan, that is angina."

I rejected this diagnosis. There was no chest clutching and I was fine when the discomfort passed. I didn't even bother to call the doctor until a couple of days later. Swifter than I could imagine, I was in the hospital. I was sure everyone was overreacting. It didn't seem that serious. An angiogram showed the right artery was blocked. A stent was placed to open the artery. I was home two days later, much wiser.

The one risk factor I could not change should have been a warning flag. My father died at 60 of heart disease and my younger brother had already had his first heart attack by the time I ended up in the hospital. Those hereditary factors increased my risk by 25 percent. I celebrate Valentine's Day with a special respect for my heart!

THE FACTS OF THE MATTER:
•Heart disease kills more women than all cancers combined. Nearly 250,000 women die of heart attacks each year compared to 43,000 women who die of breast cancer.
•Women are less likely to survive heart attacks than men.
•Stroke is a leading cause of serious, long-term disability among women.

Appeared February 13, 2002 in Kathleen and Joan's column "Double Talk" in the *Contra Costa (CA) Sun*. Recipient of the 2002 C. Everett Koop Media Award for the American Heart Association Western States Affiliate.

WILL THIS BE A COLD CYCLE?

Rebecca Kaminsky

IF YOU CAN'T LAUGH AT SOMETHING DARK, you can't live fully. Much less get through a serious illness. My mom's breast cancer hit us hard and fast. One minute I was on the phone in Berkeley talking to my mom in Wisconsin: "Honey, there is something I need to tell you." And the next minute I was on a plane to Milwaukee, anxious to meet my sister Mia and Mom's sister Joan at the airport. We flew in from all parts of the country—Mia from New York, Joan from Wyoming, and me from California.

Immediately the jealousies and jockeying for position set in. Who was going to get to take care of Mom and be in charge? Joan was the first logical choice because she is Mom's sister and her peer. I am the older of the two daughters, but my driving phobia was in high gear in this anxious situation, so I couldn't help with many of the day-to-day errands and chores. Mia is the younger sister and she was the most scared, but we all had a deep need to take some control over the uncontrollable. So in spite of the obvious answer that Joan, because of her seniority and experience, should take the lead, I was firmly convinced I was by far the most mature candidate and Mia was equally convinced that she was the most capable. At the hospital we tried our best to take care of Mom. However, behind the scenes and away from her, the three of us fought bitterly (well, Mia and I fought and Joan attempted to referee) over the details of who would get to do what: who would get to see her first when she came out of surgery, whether her first drink after 24 hours of not eating should be Coca Cola or a Popsicle, whether we should be quiet during her recovery or amuse her with funny anecdotes.

The waiting room became a refuge from this bickering. My grandparents and several of Mom's friends were there, and we didn't want to fight in front of them. We played cards, traded recipes, and tried to keep our minds from wandering to worst-case scenarios. Fortunately most of us have a sense of humor, so we attempted to tell funny stories and lighten up the atmosphere. Mia's longtime best friend Leslie had just begun her residency, so she showed up at the waiting room to give advice and help out. When the night nurse we hired for Mom walked in, my 90-year-old grandmother pulled her aside and pointed at Leslie, saying proudly, "See that cute little girl in the red sweater? She's a doctor!"

We quickly sobered up when the surgeon walked in. He announced that he'd gotten all the cancer and the three lymph nodes he took were negative from preliminary testing. She was one of the lucky ones. Moments before the room had been lively with chatter. Suddenly we were all crying. I had never seen anyone in that room cry except my sister. It was a measure of our extreme relief. Everyone in that room relied—and still relies—on Mom to keep our close-knit circle of family and friends together. She is at the heart of all of us.

When the three of us got home that night after the lumpectomy (Mom would stay in the hospital for two more days), we were exhausted. We entered the house through the garage into the laundry room. The first thing Mia did was march up to the laundry machine and strip naked, putting her coat on for modesty. She plopped her dirty clothes into the machine and turned it on. I immediately followed suit, laughing because Mia looked like a bizarre combination of dead-ass tired and a perky burlesque dancer; and I was now a mirror image. I wanted to wash the hospital grime off too. Joan had parked the car, and then walked in to find Mia and me giggling, naked under our coats. She took one look at us and deadpanned, "Will this be a cold cycle?" Then she took off her pants and sweater and dropped them in the machine. We laughed so hard that we started crying again. The realization that we were home and able to clean up while Mom was still in the hospital recovering called for laughter in order for us to take it all in.

In that humorous moment we were able to forgive each other for our regressions and fears and gain the strength to go back the next day and help Mom through her difficult recovery. We didn't stop bickering behind the scenes. After all, we still had important decisions to make, like what kind of cookies she would want at home to ease the nausea and who would do the best job helping her bathe and wash her hair. It was near impossible to stop trying to control the uncontrollable, but because we were able to laugh at ourselves, we got through it.

TREE CELLS

Ellen Hauptli

MY SISTER HOLLY ALWAYS STRUGGLED with her decision whether to be an artist or a scientist. She finally went on to study for a Ph.D. in plant genetics. Throughout her life she has overlaid her scientific interests with her artistic drive, most often in textile design. Our mother has a large batiked fabric in her kitchen of a huge wasp alighting on a yellow flower amid many other flowers. There's a Holly-made quilt in the guest room of silk-screened cranes. Mom, Holly, and I each have identical batiks of beautiful blue flowers. Holly devised a way to make an edition of three all at once. Everything is anatomically correct—she likes to depict life as she knows it from her studies, photos, and observation.

Twenty-two years ago for Christmas, Holly gave me three yards of batiked cotton: mustard, orange, and white roundish shapes with a delicate syrupy network holding it all together. It was a microscope's view of tree cells. I loved the fabric—orange was a particular favorite at that time. I immediately made it into a maxi-skirt and short jacket that I wore and wore. My boyfriend Eric once saw me from afar wearing it and hoped the flashy lady was coming his way. As the distance between us diminished, he was happy to see it was me.

Because it was such a precious piece of goods, I made sure to sew the outfit especially well. When I applied for my first job in Berkeley, one that involved engineering and constructing caftans from beautiful handwoven Middle Eastern fabrics, I brought the garment made from Holly's fabric as the example of my ability. I got the job. Working there fundamentally changed the way I perceived cutting, fitting, and sewing. No paper patterns were used. A person's body measurements interfaced with the geometric components of the caftan. Actually, my thinking was so altered that it set me on the course toward the methods I use today in my clothing design business. I thank Holly.

After a few years of wearing the tree-cell skirt, the styles and my color preferences changed. This special garment was folded carefully, wrapped, and put away to await some future transformation. I finally married Eric. Designing clothing became an avocation and vocation. Holly received her Ph.D., became a scientist for a genetic engineering firm. She worked with crop plants: corn, wheat, and her specialty, amaranth, a grain unusually high in complete protein that the Aztecs cultivated.

About ten years ago Holly was diagnosed with multiple sclerosis. One of her symptoms is optic neuritis, a visual white-out that occurs when she gets overheated by being out in the hot sun. Working outside among the plants she loves has been curtailed. Dreams of becoming an amaranth seed supplier are out of the question. Holly seems to be back at the crossroads at which she once paused. This time she's taking the other turn, the only one left marked "safe to proceed." She has outfitted herself with her very own studio, and proposes to pursue artwork now, instead of science.

I recently found my old tree-cell garment. I had taken the jacket apart long ago. The jacket leftovers were carefully tucked into the skirt, waiting. The flat pieces still bear the needle holes around the edges. Some years ago I was commissioned to hand-make and bind a special journal and used the former sleeves to cover the book. Another few pieces were juxtaposed with handwoven cotton from the Middle East and old Chinese silk ribbons in a dress that Holly, our sister Jan, and I wore for our combined five pregnancies. Yesterday I used more of the scraps along with other scraps to make a vest. Pieces of the precious handmade fabric are captured once again in a garment, held safe with seams, and framed with love for another lifetime. I don't know if Holly will ever honor me again with such a gift.

UP FOR GRABS

Linda Goldfarb

I GREW UP IN BERKELEY, CALIFORNIA so I was somewhat accustomed to odd and unusual sights. However, even my well-seasoned eyes were aghast at what I saw on this crisp fall day.

My son and I were on our way to City Rock, an indoor rock-climbing gym about half an hour from our house. We always took the freeway, except for this particular Sunday in late October—fate intervened and we drove on the city streets instead. I was driving peacefully along, lost in my thoughts, when I saw a young woman, both arms held high in the air, standing in the traffic lane on the corner of Ashby and San Pablo Avenues. As the light changed to green, I watched in horror as the oncoming traffic began moving toward her. She was holding something up in the air and waving it at the cars. It looked as if she was trying to flag them down using the object in her hands. The cars veered around her as she stood her ground.

"Look at that woman, what's she trying to do?" I exclaimed to my son.

"I think she's holding some kind of animal in the air" was his astonished reply. "Hey Mom, what are you doing?" he asked as I made an abrupt U-turn.

"I can't believe she's actually doing that to an animal. Who would do something like that?" I said as I sped back toward the intersection.

I've always been a softy for animals. I still vividly remember the day my mother took me to a department store and said she'd buy me a toy. My seven-year-old excitement at getting a present for no special reason had me searching for just the right "pet" since I was not allowed any live pets of my own. I spotted a row of majestic lions, their delicate golden coats shining under the fluorescent lights of the store. I went over to take a closer look. One lioness was not in line with the others of her species but was carelessly tossed toward the back of the shelf. She stared at me through one eye, a small bit of white fluff coming out of the socket where the other eye should have been. I gingerly picked her up and looked into her sad, yet proud, one-eyed face.

"I found what I want," I said, my eyes wide and hopeful as I ran up to my mother carrying the velvety lioness.

"Oh, at least get one that doesn't have a defect," my mother said matter-of-factly.

"No, I want this one," I pleaded as my eyes began to fill with tears. I knew no one else would buy this poor misbegotten creature and that made me want it all the more. Resigned, my mother walked me up to the counter, and I gently placed the lioness on the glass case across from the sales register.

"I guess we'll take this one," my mother said, rolling her eyes at the sales clerk.

Somehow, as an adult, I have managed to pass down my weakness (I prefer to call it "fondness") for animals to my children. So when I told my son that I had to see what the woman was trying to do with the animal, he nodded and smiled knowingly at me as we headed back in her direction.

I pulled over to the curb and we got out. The animal she was waving in the air was indeed a very small, very terrified puppy.

"What are you doing?" I asked her as calmly as possible.

"Trying to find him a home. . . want him? He's up for grabs." She then shoved him towards me. "He's going to stay small, probably not get to be more than 20 pounds."

The puppy looked up at me with large brown eyes that were surrounded by a furl of even darker brown lashes; he whimpered as I tried to cradle him in my arms. Each time I moved him to try to make him comfortable, he cried out.

"I think there might be something wrong with his leg," she mumbled.

"What do you mean? What happened to him?" I asked. There were no visible signs of injury, but he was clearly in pain.

"I don't know, I think someone might have stepped on him" was her nonchalant reply.

That was enough for me, then the logical side of my brain kicked in. We already had a large dog whom we'd adopted and, on more than one occasion when I mentioned getting a "pal" for our dog, my husband had made his position quite clear: "No more dogs. One is too many, two is out of the question." Then I looked over at my son, his eyes wide and hopeful, petting the puppy now dozing in my arms.

"You know we can't keep him," I said emphatically. Well, somewhat emphatically.

"But he's hurt," he said, his eyes beginning to fill with tears.

"We'll take him, but we can't keep him. We'll take him to a vet and get him fixed up, then we'll have to find him a home. We can't keep him," I reiterated more for myself than for him.

"We'll take him," I said to the woman. "Do you know what kind of dog it is?"

"Jack Russell terrier mix. He won't get too big," she said anxiously.

I had seen a few Jack Russell terriers—spry, perky little dogs, just like Eddie on the television show *Frasier*. Great size, quite a complement to our large husky-shepherd mix, I found myself thinking.

It was now after 5:00 on a Sunday afternoon. "We'll have to take him to the Emergency Veterinary Clinic, our vet won't be open," I told my son.

The clinic took him in right away. X-rays revealed a badly fractured right leg. Payment up front was the protocol. The call had to be made.

"You're where?" screeched my bewildered husband.

Fortunately, there had been "full disclosure" prior to our nuptials. He knew my penchant for animals and had a kind enough heart to understand. Although I promised to try to find the puppy a home immediately, we both knew that this wounded puppy hobbling on three legs had already found a home.

That was fourteen months ago. Today, our sweet "Ashby" weighs in at a healthy 52 pounds. Although at times he walks with his right leg in a ballerina's turnout, he has recovered remarkably. Our older dog dotes over Ashby like an anxious mother, and my husband has adjusted quite well; he will even admit that perhaps two dogs are better than one. I have noticed, however, that whenever our son needs a ride to City Rock, my husband insists on driving—and they always take the freeway.

Appeared in *Pet Companion* (Feb.-Mar. 1996); *North Bay Pets* (Fall 1996); *Authors* (Sept. 1996); *Dogs Today* [U.K.] (Nov. 1996); *Wry Bred* (Spring 1997); *Mr. Handyperson* (1997 vol. 5, #3); *Good Dog!* (Jan.-Feb. 1997); *Berkeley Bark* (Fall 1997).

HOW MAY I HELP YOU AND MYSELF?

Robin Slovak

June 10, 1997
Dear Dr. Slovak:
I just wanted you to know that the ulcer on my leg finally healed after I went to a special wound clinic. Thank you just the same for your care.

AS A FULLY-FLEDGED DERMATOLOGIST in practice for nine years, I was quietly mortified. Mrs. L., my former patient, was a gaunt, anxious, gray-haired woman with an autoimmune disease that caused the breakdown of her skin. I dreaded her appointments because everything I did caused her pain without improvement.

After her letter, I never saw Mrs. L. again, but I owe her an account of its legacy for my patients and me. My failure to help heal her goaded me to learn more. She is the most memorable of my patients who have inspired me to become a better doctor.

Five years after that letter, I am the dermatologist on a multidisciplinary wound team that meets monthly to consult on patients like Mrs. L. The team, which includes a plastic surgeon, a general surgeon, highly trained nurses, a physical therapist, a nutritionist, and a social worker, sees the patients as a group and then makes recommendations for ongoing care. We are the flagship clinic of this kind for our HMO in northern California. We've had some astounding successes as well as some humbling failures in helping people heal.

Many of the histories and social situations of our patients are heartrending and daunting. Some of my medical colleagues are only too happy to refer these challenging patients to us and wonder at my choice to be part of this team. Initially I was exhausted after the four-hour clinic despite having seen only three or four patients. I had not seen wounds and ulcers of this magnitude before and was shocked to find out that people lived with them for years. I felt as if I had gone back to school when I first joined the wound team. It was foreign territory for me when it came to evaluating a pressure ulcer or applying a pressure dressing.

But had our clinic existed when I was seeing Mrs. L., I would not have even been on the team because I had some healing of my own to do. I was struggling with despair, overwork, and burnout. My healing was emotional and first required acknowledgement of the angst I had carried from childhood as a young girl and later as an adult. The only daughter in a family of ten, I had difficulty saying with conviction that I had reached my limit, especially in situations where I could be of help. Instead of being more sure-footed as I finished my medical training and gained experience, I felt more ambivalent, more burdened, more reluctant to accept challenges. Perhaps psychic wounds would be more impressive if they were visible. Help came from many places not recognized by me as helpful at the outset. My healing was incremental. I was fortunate to have my own mentors and sages along the way: a yoga teacher, a therapist, friends with whom I could bare my soul, my daughter and my husband, a brother, a cat and a dog, and many of my patients.

In college I thought that my greatest hurdle would be the stiff competition to be accepted to medical school and then into desirable postgraduate training programs; I wasn't prepared for the long, stressful hours and years of training, with the lack of restorative personal time and chronic delayed gratification that create conditions that can be injurious to the soul, any soul. Sleep deprivation, a given in our train-ing, can also be a form of torture. A close friend said that it took a year for her to recover from the sleep deprivation she endured during her internal medicine residency. I felt battered by those experiences and reluctant to speak up for fear of ridicule. When I trained, despite the feminist movement, women had to prove themselves deserving of a medical education.

I was ambivalent about the process of becoming a doctor. In the mid-'70s, during my third year of medical school, I was on a ski weekend with three friends who had just finished their internship when the question came up: "How much would you have to be paid to repeat your internship year?" The consensus was between $500,000 and $1,000,000. An intern's salary then was less than $10,000. I was in awe of those friends who are still among the brightest people I know. I wasn't certain that I could measure up or give up that much time in my life. After I finished my internship, I decided that I could not be paid enough to do it again.

I learned to compartmentalize experiences that were too painful to look at right then so that I could continue to do what needed to be done. Eventually my patients and I paid a price for this unprocessed emotional homework, which can be experienced as lack of kindness or compassion. As Rachel Naomi Remen says about physicians in *Kitchen Table Wisdom*, in order to learn objectivity to help their patients with painful events, they distance themselves from their own wounds and that distancing blocks their healing. An essential part of my psychic healing has been willingness to forgive myself for my limitations and to move on.

Many physicians and nurses suffer from prolonged burnout—some of them are my friends. Because of a taboo about talking about one's own needs and despair with the current state of medical practice, we feel isolated and stuck. Twelve years ago I was in dire straits. As one of my colleagues said, "People who don't care, don't burn out." I was practicing in a situation in which I felt like a cog in a health-care machine. Moreover, I had done this to myself. I had signed on with a large, nonprofit managed-care group after doing an extensive search of the private sector in the Bay Area. I soon saw that this dermatology clinic was a toxic environment, evidenced by constant turnover of the staff at all levels. The chief of the clinic was ambitious at the expense of his colleagues. He held us to an untenable standard of practice: a new patient every ten minutes. Patients with warts were scheduled for five minutes when most needed at least ten. The senior physicians, who were partners, kept their heads down. I was new, on track to become a partner, and conscious of my probationary status; I felt I had to comply.

One of the partners became my confidante. Older and experienced, she was not afraid to speak up on the physicians' behalf, but her comments went unheeded in our meetings. She was deft at working the system, contriving to work with only the best medical assistants and more skilled than I in negotiating with patients whose expectations could not be addressed in one appointment. I floundered. Eventually the human resources department intervened, and the tyrant moved on. Our new chief, who had risen through the ranks, was a model of integrity and an excellent clinician. Under his influence, the department moved toward more sustainable practice, but our respite was short-lived.

The parade of demands and changes was unremitting as our organization struggled to adjust to the rapidly evolving health-care market in the '90s. For months, doctors were asked to work ten-hour days to catch up on our backlog of patients, which we did. As there was an insufficient number of physicians, the backlog recurred. We took a pay cut.

My contacts with my patients were not rewarding, and they often seemed dissatisfied as well. I felt dehumanized by the pressures to do more in less time. Patients came with the "dreaded list" of itemized problems that they hoped to discuss during the visit. We salvaged our tattered sense of dignity by saving the most outrageous ones to show each other and whoop with laughter over the impossibility of doing them justice—a form of medical black humor that had gotten us through hard times before. At my lowest point during my years at the clinic, I would lie down on a blanket on the floor of my office and sleep during my lunch hour. As the day passed and I felt more stressed, my voice became hoarse. I drank water or tea constantly to soothe my throat. My sense of humor and the absurd abandoned me. I felt so pressured for time that I inadvertently hurt myself—slamming my fingers in metal filing cabinets and hitting my shins against the examining table, unconscious punishment for feeling so negative. No matter how I tried to look on the bright side, I felt only despair. To have trained so hard to end up where I was seemed like a wicked fate. And in a way it was tragic. I was fortunate in many ways, but couldn't see it.

Meanwhile, my home was not the sanctuary I needed. I was unofficially trying to win the errand marathon. With a doctor husband and a small child I adored, I repeatedly demanded more of myself than was reasonable. My husband, an academic oncologist insulated from the clinical pressures I faced, listened to my unceasing complaints—a true test of his devotion. I sensed it was vital that I do something, because my unhappiness was poisonous to me and those I loved.

I've always been a seeker and open to new experiences. It's one of the characteristics that I like about myself and it became essential to my recovery. Clearly, I wasn't going to feel better on my own. Help in recovering from my desperate state came from many directions. I had dabbled at yoga for many years. My teacher was a paragon of joyful energy, and my yoga class became more meaningful as a realm where I focused only on the present moment. I loved Śavāsana—a resting, meditative pose in which I lay on the floor eyes closed at the end of class. I could sense the tension in my joints, muscles, and throat leaking out and evaporating into thin air. I began to see a therapist who was kind, patient, and insistent that I take better care of myself. At first I was bewildered; no one had ever said that to me. She was appropriately incensed on my behalf by the circumstances under which I practiced. I needed that validation. I had lost my sense of perspective and felt progressively more overwhelmed. I understood little about nurturing my inner self, but much about self-preservation—little about savoring life rather than just surviving it.

My therapist was an advocate for me against my most critical inner self—a counterpoint to that mean and increasingly bitter voice as disappointment with the quality of my life grew. I had chosen a vocation of "helping others" because I felt validated, but I hadn't counted on feeling depleted by an unending stream of patients. My mother, a paragon of self-sacrifice and stoicism, was my model. Growing up I was always in the service of others—usually my brothers who were younger than I. Gradually I overcame my fear of facing my own needs and realized I must nurture myself as well.

About five years ago, help for me and other doctors became available on the job. I signed up for courses offered through my employer on stress management, communication skills, and most recently an ongoing program using yoga and meditation to deflect stress. These are special classes for MDs. Finally, here was public acknowledgement of what I'd experienced in private. A program entitled Physician Wellness was created after doctors in greater numbers than ever before stopped working because of disabilities attributed to stress.

The stress management course met at lunchtime. We doctors joked that it was an additional pressure just to show up, because we usually caught up on charting, telephone calls, and prescription refills at lunch as we downed our sandwiches. The communication course lasted five days and featured actors who would take the patient's role and then join in with other MDs in small groups for feedback about what worked and what bothered them. It took courage for me to get up in front of my colleagues and flounder—and I did. I said that often I did not feel like a physician; instead, I was a lesion technician on an assembly line, asked many times each day to identify and remove various growths. There was insufficient time to get to know my patients. My pent-up anger was a barrier that I had to scale with each appointment. The residue of previous unhappy interactions hindered all future encounters; negative self-talk kicked in when I felt exploited by a patient whose requests went beyond my tolerance. For example, I would frequently be asked to see a relative in the same visit, "Can't you just work him in, Doc? It takes so long to get an appointment." I'd be asked this despite already running 45 minutes late. In the communication workshop I had a chance to work through my anger, which when defused allowed me to learn to be calm in the face of one more excessive demand.

At the moment I am taking part in an ongoing class of yoga, meditation, and discussion modeled on psychologist Jon Kabat-Zinn's stress reduction clinic for patients at the University of Massachusetts Medical Center. This is an intensive eight-week course for physicians followed by monthly practice sessions. The inner serenity that I practice in and out of the class follows me to the clinic. Now when I see a patient with a long list, I take a deep breath and experience a few seconds of Śavāsana before asking, "How may I help you?"

Working with a team in the wound clinic to treat what some consider hopeless problems, where we support each other and learn as we go along, has relieved the sense of isolation I felt with Mrs. L. Best of all, I am now able to see that my patients give something back to me as I help them. Daily there are people who are memorable for the grace, wit, and courage with which they face life's blows. It's as if scales have fallen from my eyes. I am honored to be a healer for them.

CONTRIBUTORS

Born in Italy, RINA ALCALAY grew up in Argentina and Chile. At 26 she came to the United States and earned her M.A. in Education and Ph.D. in Communication at Stanford. She taught at UCLA and UC Davis, specializing in cross-cultural and international health communication and publishing widely in this area. Rina lives in Berkeley with her husband and two children, 14 and 21.

SUSAN ANTOLIN spent three years in Japan, where she fell in love with modern Japanese poetry. She is a nonpracticing attorney and mother of three young children living in Walnut Creek, where she writes in grocery store parking lots, at red lights, and in the occasional quiet of her kitchen.

Born and raised in Mankato, MN, JUNE ANNE BAKER earned a sociology degree from Arizona State, a Master's in Regional and City Planning from the University of Oklahoma, and a law degree from UC Berkeley. In 1970 she moved to San Francisco, and became a founding member of Bay Area Women Planners. June turned to writing in her forties, and was a charter member of this workshop. She died of cancer in 2000, at 53.

WENDY SCOTT BERTRAND considers herself a Californian with one foot on French soil, where she started her architectural career and where she travels often. She joined the Fall 2002 Writing Workshop to launch the memoir of her three-decade voyage as an architect and manager in Federal Service. She writes in Del Norte County (near the Oregon border) and in San Francisco.

JENNA BUFFALOE never did get a job. Instead, she moved to Oakland, met a wild cowboy who didn't mind supporting her, and settled down to write her memoirs.

RONNIE CAPLANE is a reformed lawyer turned freelance writer. She has a weekly column in the *Piedmonter* and *Montclarion*, and is a frequent contributor to the *Jewish Bulletin of Northern California*. Her articles have also appeared in the *Chicago Tribune, Detroit Free Press, Cleveland Plain Dealer, Denver Post, San Francisco Recorder*, and various Jewish newspapers throughout the country.

A psychologist with a string of academic publications on children and family issues, CHARLI DEPNER planned to spend some of her maternity leave knocking off a book about adopting her daughters from Russia. The writing workshop inspired her to pursue "writing from the heart." Her life has been blessed by the gift of this workshop and the warm, creative, and inspiring women she met there.

Former social worker NANCY DEUTSCH has taught journal writing, poetry, and oral history for the last 12 years. She's currently a California Arts Council Artist-in-Residence directing intergenerational writing programs in the public schools and low-income housing. Nancy is the author/editor of *Voices of Our Own—Mothers, Daughters, and Elders of the Tenderloin Tell Their Stories* (2002). Visit www.frommywindowbooks.com for more information.

DIANA DIVECHA is a developmental psychologist and former chair of the Department of Interdisciplinary Studies in Human Development at Sonoma State University. After many years of teaching students about child development, she stepped out of academia to enjoy her own daughters, now 11 and 14.

BONNIE EPSTEIN is a cancer survivor whose choice to use acupuncture as a healing tool has enriched her life in ways never imagined. Her acupuncturist is her life-teacher. Bonnie now embraces impermanence, lives in the moment, and laughs a lot. She is a retired psychotherapist who devotes her time to writing, gardening, and animal rescue.

KATHLEEN FARADAY has lived in the Philippines, Australia, Korea, and Hong Kong and all across the U.S. from Winnemucca, Nevada and Boise, Idaho to New York and Alabama. Piano and golf lessons, hiking, biking, skiing, and cooking are squeezed in between her job as an account manager at Nichols Institute Diagnostics, time with her grandchildren, and co-writing a column, "Double Talk," for the *Contra Costa Sun*.

ELIZABETH FISHEL is the author of four books—*Sisters, The Men in Our Lives, I Swore I'd Never Do That*, and *Reunion*. She has also written widely for magazines including *Vogue, Oprah's O, Redbook, Parents, Family Circle*, and *The New York Times Book Review*, and was a Contributing Editor at *Child*. In addition to her Wednesday Writers' Workshop, she has taught writing at UC Berkeley Extension for many years. She lives in Oakland with her husband and two sons.

Born in Pueblo, CO, DIAN GILLMAR worked as a corporate librarian while rearing two daughters. When the younger went off to college, she became development director for Brown University's West Coast office, where she worked for ten years. Dian has kept a daily journal for 20 years, and since her retirement has been writing poetry. She is an attentive grandmother to two boys and two girls.

LINDA GOLDFARB is a paralegal/writer turned vintner. She and her husband Steve own Anomaly Vineyards, a small cabernet-producing winery in California's Napa Valley. In addition to the winery, Linda is also involved with the local animal shelter and has three dogs that keep her quite busy. Linda's son, Chris, attends UC Davis, and her daughter, Emilie, is an actress in Los Angeles.

MICHELLE WELLS GRANT, a native Californian of 43 years, currently lives in Austin, Texas with her husband Mike and daughter Elizabeth. Michelle can't get enough of the creative life and enjoys writing, sewing, jewelry-making, and drawing. She has just completed her first children's picture book, entitled *Patches*.

ELLEN HAUPTLI crafts simple, elegant, fun clothing for women of all ages and sizes in Berkeley, California. Her very supportive family—husband, daughter, and son—also lets her play a lot of softball there.

Born in Brooklyn and raised on Long Island, TERRI HINTE has lived in the Bay Area since 1973. An avid gardener and a lifelong student of languages and metaphysics, she has worked as a publicist and editor in the music business for nearly 30 years, and is a frequent traveler to Brazil. Her writing has appeared in *Travelers' Tales Brazil* and *Passionfruit* magazine.

REBECCA KAMINSKY has a Master of Arts in liberal studies with a concentration in women's studies from the City University of New York Graduate Center. She lives and writes in Berkeley. Her main goal as a mom is to instill in her son a healthy appreciation for candy, television, and occasionally organic food.

SUZANNE LAFETRA spent her twenties in Mexico, where she developed a taste for altars and folk art. She currently lives in Berkeley and tends a garden filled with persimmons and marigolds. She writes after her husband and two small children have gone to bed.

ANN LIPSON is an immigration lawyer, born in England, who, after raising triplets, now age 29, divides her time, with her husband, between Berkeley and their renovated farmhouse in the Loire valley of France. There they grow fruit and vegetables in the *potager*, and indulge their passion for all things French.

LORNA C. MASON edited and published *But What, My Dear, Do You Know About Hotels?*, a collection of the reminiscences of Flora Gellatly Means, a Colorado rancher's wife and Lorna's maternal grandmother. The book was, Lorna wrote, "an act of love." The mother of a son and a daughter, Lorna was 59 at the time of her death from breast cancer in 1997.

ELIZABETH A. MONTGOMERY, a retired bank marketing executive, writer, wife, mother, and eight-year breast cancer survivor, lives in Berkeley. She is grateful for the support she received from her friends, family, and colleagues after her diagnosis of breast cancer, and thanks everyone who is putting time and money into conquering this disease.

MARY-JO MURPHY, a Connecticut native, is a Health Educator and Registered Nurse. From her father she learned a love of people-watching, from her mother a love of words. These sensibilities allow her to tune into life's dramas, themes, and truths, endless subjects to be shaped into essays, novels, picture books, screenplays, or long, therapeutic journal entries. Her greatest pleasure as a writer is to elicit an emotional response.

LINDA JOY MYERS, Ph.D., M.F.T., is the author of *Becoming Whole: Writing Your Healing Story*. Linda combines her knowledge and experience as a therapist with her writing skills to teach memoir-as-healing classes. "The Music Man" is excerpted from *Don't Call Me Mother*, a memoir about transcending a pattern of mother-daughter abandonment to find forgiveness and compassion.

KARA JANE ROLLINS is a Bay Area therapist and writer who grew up in Nebraska, Wyoming, and Montana and moved to San Francisco in the mid-1960s. Kara likes to write about the West and about life experiences.

LORI ROSENTHAL lives in the Oakland hills with her husband David and two daughters. She thanks all three of them for supplying endless source material and for being willing to see their names and stories in print. Lori urges all readers to make time for annual medical check-ups and recommended tests.

CAROLE SIRULNICK, Ph.D., is a clinical psychologist in private practice for almost 30 years. She received a B.A. in journalism at New York University in 1971. Currently at work on a book about a Sherpa from the Himalayas of Nepal, Carole has contributed to Adair Lara's *Slowing Down in a Speeded Up World* and to various small Bay Area publications.

MARTHA SLAVIN has spent the last five years living in Japan and France as a trailing spouse, trying to meet the challenges of new languages and cultures while maintaining a stable family environment. She continues her cyclical life as artist, teacher, writer, wife, mother, and community worker, but her experiences as an expat are now the focus of her writing. Her son Ted is 13.

ROBIN SLOVAK practices dermatology in the East Bay. She has traveled around the world and loves her native California all the more for it. Under the nom de plume Robin Lawrence, she co-wrote a column, "Double Talk," for the *Contra Costa Sun*. On her days off she hikes, gardens, and cooks with family and friends. Robin is a docent at the marvelous Ruth Bancroft Garden in Walnut Creek. Her bedside table is overflowing with books.

JOAN STEVENSON completed her college degree as a single working mother. When she remarried, three more children came with their father, like the Brady Bunch without Alice. Writing provides an outlet amid the joys and chaos of raising six children and caring for an aging parent. When Robin Lawrence retired from writing the column "Double Talk" in the *Contra Costa Sun*, Joan joined Kathleen Faraday as co-columnist.

INES SWANEY enjoys writing about her daily encounters and adventures in the field of language, where she works as a Spanish interpreter, translator, and voiceover talent. A native of Venezuela, she has now lived in California longer than anywhere else. She started UC Berkeley at age 16 and graduated with a Bachelor of Architecture degree.

Born and raised in Bombay, SHAHNAZ CHINOY TAPLIN works in public interest communications. Specifically, she conducts mass media campaigns for foundations, nonprofits in the Bay Area, and NGO's in India. Her focus is on women's issues, adoption/foster care, environment, and more recently Diaspora philanthropy.

GINA WALDMAN lectures widely on college campuses on the issue of terrorism. She is the former director of the Bay Area Council for Rescue and Renewal, an organization dedicated to helping secure freedom for Jews and dissidents in the former Soviet Union. In 1992, Gina was awarded the Martin Luther King, Jr. Humanitarian Award for her work on human rights. She is the founder of Jimena (Jews Indigenous to the Middle East and North Africa, www.jimena-justice.org).

ANNE ZIEBUR came to live in the United States in 1959 via her native Denmark, then Belgium and Spain. In addition to homemaking and child-rearing, she has practiced writing and photography for many years. She recently discovered the magic of painting and delights in sharing her newfound joys with her young grandchildren.